Social Skills in Pictures, Stories, and Songs

A Multisensory Program
for Preschool and
Early Elementary Students

Teacher's Guide

Loretta A. Serna ● **M. Elizabeth Nielsen** ● **Steven R. Forness**

Research Press • 2612 North Mattis Avenue • Champaign, Illinois 61822 • (800) 519-2707 • www.researchpress.com

Composition by Jeff Helgesen
Cover design by Linda Brown, Positive I.D. Graphics, Inc.
Printed by Malloy, Inc.

The *Social Skills in Pictures, Stories, and Songs* program may be ordered from the publisher at the address given on the title page. The complete program consists of this Teacher's Guide and music CD, a Storybook, and ten copies of each of four coloring books (one for each story character).

Complete program

   ISBN-13: 978–0-87822–575–7
   ISBN-10: 0–87822–575–0

Additional sets of coloring books

   ISBN-13: 978–0-87822–579–8
   ISBN-10: 0–87822–579-X

Library of Congress Catalog Number 2006905461 (Teacher's Guide)

To the memory of Irene G. Serna and to Dennis Higgins and Hill Walker —
our heroes, who were always there when needed

Contents

Foreword

I am extremely impressed with this curricular program for teaching critically important social skills to young children who need mastery of them in order to succeed in school. I can think of no more important task than the effective teaching of such skills in natural settings (home, school, community) in which the teaching-learning process is carefully embedded in ongoing, daily routines. Long-term research shows that such skills-based programs can prevent the later development of a host of destructive outcomes, including violent delinquent acts, heavy drinking, teenage pregnancy, low achievement, school failure and dropout, and severe behavioral episodes in school (Hawkins, Catalano, Kosterman, Abbott, & Hill, 1999). Programs that teach specific skills that allow children and youth to cope more effectively with the challenges and demands of their daily lives are the ones that make a long-term difference in overall quality of life.

When children begin their school careers, they are required to make important social-behavioral adjustments in two areas: They must negotiate healthy relationships with both teachers and peers. Failure in either of these domains puts children or youth at some degree of risk for failure in school; lack of success in both domains is associated with school dropout and other destructive outcomes. It is essential that all students get off to the best possible start to their school careers.

Social Skills in Pictures, Stories, and Songs (SSPSS) is a superb tool for accomplishing this task. It begins by targeting the skill domains that key stakeholders (teachers, parents, administrators) indicate are most important for children to master as they begin schooling. The skill areas targeted by the SSPSS program are also validated by a large number of studies reported in the literature on the correlates of school success. The authors have constructed this elegant curriculum so that it fits seamlessly into the instructional scope and sequence of early childhood and kindergarten settings, indicating their awareness of the dynamics of the teaching-learning process. Reading the SSPSS materials leaves one with the inescapable impression that these authors are masters of instruction and skills acquisition "from the ground up" and that they have a thorough grasp of the key instructional principles that produce sound outcomes for diverse groups of learners.

I was privileged to observe the research and development of the SSPSS during the time my colleagues and I were part of the Head Start Mental Health Research Consortium, a collaborative effort of the U.S.

Administration on Children, Youth, and Families and the National Institute of Mental Health. This unique alliance gave university researchers the opportunity to participate as part of the consortium in developing and evaluating assessment measures, prevention and intervention programs for young children. I can certify not only that the SSPSS program is well conceptualized, carefully designed, and instructor friendly, but also that it is one of the most carefully researched curricular programs to be introduced within any field during the last 20 years. In short, the program works, and users like it—an extremely rare achievement in the field of early intervention.

I believe the SSPSS program is a seminal and rare contribution to the instructional and social skills literature in early childhood education. I greatly admire the authors for their work and their approach, and I predict the SSPSS program will be a huge success.

HILL M. WALKER
UNIVERSITY OF OREGON:
    PROFESSOR, COLLEGE OF EDUCATION
    DIRECTOR, CENTER ON HUMAN DEVELOPMENT
    CODIRECTOR, INSTITUTE ON VIOLENCE AND DESTRUCTIVE BEHAVIOR
SENIOR RESEARCH SCIENTIST, OREGON RESEARCH INSTITUTE, EUGENE

Acknowledgments

This program and the research that accompanies it has been a collaborative project from its very beginnings. The authors are singularly indebted to our funding agencies: the U.S. Administration on Children, Youth and Families (ACYF)—particularly our project officers, Mike Lopez, Ph.D., and Louisa Tarullo, Ed.D.—and the National Institute of Mental Health (NIMH)—especially our project officers, Cheryl Boyce, Ph.D., Peter Jensen, M.D., and Kimberly Hoagwood, Ph.D. Their support and active interest in this endeavor are much appreciated. We are also indebted to our fellow members of the Head Start Mental Health Research Consortium (HSMHRC): Jeanne Brooks-Gunn, Ph.D., Lisa Berlin, Ph.D., and Lisa McCabe, Ph.D. (Columbia University); Donna Bryant, Ph.D., Janis Kupersmidt, Ph.D., and Peg Burchinal, Ph.D. (University of North Carolina); Hill Walker, Ph.D., Ed Feil, Ph.D., and Herb Severson, Ph.D. (University of Oregon); and Ann Kaiser, Ph.D., and Terry Hancock, Ph.D. (Vanderbilt University). Their feedback and encouragement are everywhere reflected in our work on this program, as is their friendship.

At the University of New Mexico, we are particularly grateful to Christine Curran, Ph.D. (now at Western Washington State University), who developed and refined our stories; to Tom Graham, B.F.A., who illustrated our stories; and to Dennis Higgins, Ph.D., who wrote both lyrics and music for the songs. Ours was probably the only ACYF research grant ever to provide funding for a story writer, musician, and an artist! Their particular brand of wizardry, coupled with their understanding of the needs of children, could not have been more effective in the completion of this project. Dennis also used this program— above and beyond the call of duty—with his special education classroom of twice-exceptional children to particular advantage.

Graduate and postgraduate trainees were indispensable to this research: Katrina Lambros, Ph.D., Scott Gullett, Ph.D., Heather Borg, Ph.D., and, especially, Daniel DeLaO, M.A., who was such an excellent preschool teacher in the *first* controlled trial that we had to do a *second* one to control for what we came to call the "Daniel Effect." Our colleagues at the University of New Mexico, Nancy Mattern, Ph.D., and Candace Shaw, Ph.D., were indispensable in data analysis.

Mary Hale, M.A., and Deborah Baca of the Youth Development Incorporated (YDI) Head Start Project in Albuquerque and their wonderful administrative staff and superb teachers and assistant teachers were the lifeblood of this project. Their professionalism, skills, and dedication were our inspiration, and they were truly our colleagues in this endeavor. Finally, our best inspiration came from the children in Head Start and their families—our efforts pale beside theirs!

Introduction

A good deal of evidence now exists to suggest not only that social-emotional development is an absolutely critical foundation for early learning but also that systematic teaching of social and emotional skills in the early years sets the stage for academic success throughout later schooling (Forness, 2005; Zins, Weissberg, Wang, & Walberg, 2004). This same evidence also suggests that such instruction in the early years may actually prevent emotional or behavioral disorders from occurring in children at risk for such disorders (Fox, Jack, & Broyles, 2005; Luby, 2006).

ABOUT THE PROGRAM

Social Skills in Pictures, Stories, and Songs is the result of a six-year project designed to help young children develop the social and emotional skills necessary to succeed in their early school years. The program combines a number of sensory modalities, using stories, mnemonics, coloring books, songs, role-playing, and visual aids. Teachers and caregivers of children in child care, preschool, and the early elementary grades can use this guide to implement a comprehensive multisensory program. They may also select specific program components or adapt them as they see fit in response to their children's particular needs. Thoroughly field tested in clinical trials and a follow-up in Head Start preschool settings, the program is also appropriate for young children in child care situations and for school-age children in the early elementary grades. An overview of the program's development and evidence base is given in Appendix A.

Pictures, Stories, and Songs

While developing the program, we recognized that teaching social and emotional skills should not necessarily be separated from daily routines at home, care settings, or school. Teaching children these types of skills may actually be more effective if the skills can be integrated into whatever naturally occurs in such settings. Such integration may well make parents, caregivers, and teachers more willing to undertake such instruction. Many mental health professionals, for example, have tried to develop programs to foster social-emotional development in child care and preschool settings but have failed because caregivers and teachers have seen such programs either as extra work or as interruptions to their daily routines. Even though they may see some value in these programs, they are not always convinced that adding on such programs is worth the effort.

With these issues in mind, we cast about for a way to make the important work of teaching social and emotional skills a more integral part of the natural caregiving and school environment. When we looked more carefully at different settings for children in their early years, the settings seemed to have in common three instructional elements: pictures, stories, and songs! Picture books, posters and other visual displays, and the like are ubiquitous in just about any care setting for young children, preschool, or elementary classroom. Stories are likewise the lifeblood of childhood, as bedtime rituals at home, storytime before afternoon naps in day care, and daily lessons in school. And most of us still fondly remember the songs from our early years: *Wheels on the Bus, The Itsy Bitsy Spider,* and other standards.

Pictures, stories, and songs not only represent wonderfully familiar opportunities in which to embed the important work of developing social and emotional competence, they also offer the possibility of *integrating* all these modalities in pursuit of a common purpose. Such a multisensory approach takes advantage of the different ways children learn. Some children, for example, might learn more readily from seeing concepts presented in pictures. Others might learn more effectively by listening to a story or, in the case of older children, reading it. Some might grasp these concepts best when hearing them presented musically and being able to sing along.

Skill Selection

Because children must master several social-emotional skills in early childhood, we decided to select those skills that teachers, parents, and administrators consider most critical to school success in the early grades. After reviewing studies in this area, we conducted a social validation study with teachers, parents, administrators, and social workers/psychologists to determine what skills were most important. The results of the literature review and social validation study indicated four critical skill areas: (a) following directions, (b) sharing, (c) managing one's own behavior, and (d) problem solving (Forness, Serna, Kavale, & Nielsen, 1998). We then developed simple mnemonics to depict and encapsulate the essential components of each skill: BEST, PALS, TEAM, and WORK. As you will see, across the stories, pictures, and songs for each of the four skills, the mnemonics not only help children remember the skill steps, but also serve as cues or reminders that teachers can use throughout the day to prompt children to use each skill when the occasion demands.

PROGRAM COMPONENTS

In addition to this teacher's guide, *Social Skills in Pictures, Stories, and Songs* includes a storybook, a music CD, and a set of four coloring books.

Storybook

The storybook presents the exploits of four animals: a roadrunner, a prairie dog, a raccoon, and a porcupine. Each story involves a different animal character and shows how that character learns to use a specific skill. The stories and their associated mnemonics are as follows:

Rosie the Roadrunner Learns to Follow Directions **(BEST)**

Prairie Dog Pete Learns to Share **(PALS)**

Roscoe the Raccoon Learns to Manage His Behavior **(TEAM)**

Prickles the Porcupine Learns to Solve Problems **(WORK)**

These stories follow a predictable format in which children are introduced to the main character, the main character's problem is defined, and the main character—with the help of friends—solves the problem by learning and using the skill. The skill of following directions (BEST) serves as a foundation for the other skills; after children learn this skill, they may learn the other skills in any order. The TEAM and WORK skills require children to develop cognitive skills along with the main social skill, however, and as such are more complex and probably best taught last.

Music CD

The music CD bound at the back of this teacher's guide includes four songs, one for each story. Each song involves one of the animal characters and presents a skill and its related mnemonic. A vocalist plays the guitar and is joined by children, who add their voices and dialogue to the songs. In addition to being used as indicated in the skill lessons, the songs can be played and sung at other times during the day, either in the group or by individual children. A song sheet, including music and lyrics, follows each set of lessons in this guide.

Coloring Books

Four separate coloring books, one corresponding to each story and skill, give children a hands-on way to assimilate the skill information. Based on the storybook illustrations, these pages show the main characters learning the skills and include captions to reinforce key ideas. The lessons suggest pages from these books for the children to color, but teachers should feel free to assign pages as appropriate for their groups and should not be limited by the drawings in the coloring books. Having the children create their own drawings is always an option.

Teacher's Guide

This teacher's guide provides specific instructional procedures in the form of skill lessons, as well as a range of supplementary materials useful in conducting the program.

Skill Lessons

Each skill is accompanied by four to six lessons. The lessons specify a range of pages in the storybook to read aloud, then use the story content as the basis for instruction. Because the instructional procedures follow the text of the stories for each skill, like the stories, the lessons also follow a predictable sequence:

1. Children are prepared for skill learning by hearing how the story characters define the skill and seeing them illustrate the need for it.

2. In a small-group or whole-class format, the teacher guides children in exploring the situations in which the skill may be useful and understanding the rationale for using the skill.

3. Children are next introduced to the specific skill steps, which are reinforced through repetition and example. The lessons include guidelines for reinforcing learning of the skill steps by having children listen to and sing the song associated with the skill.

4. The teacher models the skill steps for the children and asks them for feedback on the accuracy of skill performance. The children are next given the opportunity to role-play the skill.

It is important to note that these lessons need not be seen as a separate part of the children's daily routine—they can be applied at any time, especially during normal story times. Elsewhere, we describe how these lessons can serve as prereading or reading lessons within the general framework of literacy skills in preschool and the early grades (Serna, Nielsen, Curran, Higgins, & Forness, 2002).

Following each set of lessons are patterns for making felt board cutouts of the story's characters, whole-page displays of the skill definitions and skill steps, and song sheets.

Related Activities

Appendix B in this guide includes a number of ideas for using large-group, small-group, and individual activities in the form of learning centers to enhance skill learning and generalization. These activities include opportunities to sing the songs, make clay sculptures and puppets of the story characters, perform a puppet show for parents, and engage in additional role-playing practice. Other possibilities include playing bingo and using flash cards for review.

Role-Playing

Role-playing serves two purposes in the program: It gives students the opportunity to practice the skill steps, and it shows teachers what their students have learned. As noted previously, the lessons include a specific role-play procedure that presents the skill steps. Role-play practice also takes place incidentally, in the classroom and on the playground, as natural opportunities present themselves during the course of the day. When an opportunity for skill use presents itself (or when the teacher creates one), the teacher praises the child for using the skill appropriately or provides corrective feedback if the child missed the opportunity to use the skill or did not follow the skill steps appropriately. To provide corrective feedback, the teacher may refer to the skill stories and characters, picture cues, songs from the original lessons, previous class discussions about the skill, and other role-play experiences.

Appendix C describes the way we used role-play evaluations to measure students' skill acquisition and includes a role-play evaluation checklist for each skill.

PROGRAM IMPLEMENTATION

Caregivers or teachers may use all or part of this program, as the needs of the children in their care dictate. Field testing of the *SSPSS* program, however, included all components of the program, and thus the most effective use of the program will involve the entire series of lessons and related activities.

Most of the materials needed for these lessons and accompanying activities are included in the package for this program. Not included are a CD player to play the music CD, a felt board and felt to construct the character shapes; an easel pad or dry erase board, if appropriate; and crayons or colored markers. These items are readily available in child care and early childhood education settings, as well as in early elementary classrooms. Each child will also need a copy of the coloring book for the skill being taught. Additional art supplies are helpful in conducting additional activities to enhance skill learning activities, as specified in Appendix B. Finally, if someone can play a piano or guitar, that person can use the song sheets to contribute live musical performance.

If children are already reading, teachers may wish to present the skill definitions and component steps on posters or easel pad pages for them to read and also have children read parts of the story aloud as the lesson progresses. If children have not yet mastered reading skills, more focus can be given to the narrative and pictures. The mnemonics, pictures, and songs are thus designed to foster preliteracy and beginning reading skills.

The following pages provide some basic tips for storytelling and strategies for children who have difficulty listening. These tips apply to all of the lessons.

Storytelling Tips

1. Read and practice the story ahead of time.

2. Perform with enthusiasm and whole-hearted enjoyment.

3. Keep your eyes on the audience most of the time.

4. Be certain that all the children can see the pictures.

5. Repeat important phrases, ask questions, or say things in another way.

6. Allow children to ask questions as you read.

7. Help children pay attention by having them participate and move about.

8. Stick to the lesson plan outline at each story time.

9. Use props, gestures, and different voices; vary your tone and pace.

10. Be very careful to model the skill correctly.

11. Smile! Smile! Smile!

12. Ask, "What do you think is going to happen next?"

13. Call on children by name to avoid group chaos.

14. Employ plenty of expression when reading.

15. Read slowly enough for the children to create mental pictures of what they have just heard.

16. Change your tone to fit the dialogue.

17. Modify your pace to fit the story.

Strategies for Children Who Have Difficulty Listening

1. Have the student sit near you so you can offer assistance in paying attention.

2. Keep distractions away (toys, books, noise from the hall).

3. Stick to the lesson plan so the child knows what to expect.

4. Work audience participation into the story (fill in the blanks, movement, props).

5. Ask questions during the story to keep the child thinking and involved.

6. When explaining, speak close, make eye contact, and be sure the child looks at you.

7. Before each story time, speak individually and privately to the child about what will be happening in order to motivate listening. Say, for example, "Watch for Rosie and see if she wins the race" or "I want to make sure you are in a good place to see and hear every word of this story because something silly is going to happen."

8. During story time, give the child positive feedback (a smile, pat, praise) for paying attention.

9. Use a volunteer to act as the child's "private tutor." The tutor sits near the child at story time and quietly prompts the child's attention and asks questions to keep the child involved.

10. Establish a few clear (but not strict) rules for story time. State the rules in a positive way, focusing on the alternatives to restless behavior. For instance, you could say, "You have to be sitting down and be quiet enough for everyone else to hear."

11. Establish a consequence for not following the story time rules. Give one reminder, then follow through with the consequence.

12. Make the story as entertaining and exciting as possible.

Following Directions

Rosie the Roadrunner

SKILL DEFINITION

Following Directions means that you listen, understand,
and do what someone has asked you to do.

SKILL STEPS

B   **Body** straight, hands on your lap, and feet on the floor.

E   **Eyes** on the speaker.

S   **Serious** face.

T   **Turn** your body toward the speaker.

NOTE

Let children know that they should follow directions only from people they know and trust, not from strangers or from people who might tell them to do something they know is wrong (for example, stealing).

L E S S O N   1

<table>
<tr>
<td>In this lesson, children meet Rosie, Rosie's mom, and Lou the Lizard and learn the definition of Following Directions.</td>
<td>In Lesson 2, children are introduced to the mnemonic **BEST**.</td>
</tr>
</table>

TEACHING GUIDE

Introduce the skill by letting students know that today they will begin learning about Rosie the Roadrunner and the skill of Following Directions.

1. Read pages 1–11 in the storybook.

2. Review this part of the story for comprehension, using the felt board and cutouts. Ask:

   Who are the characters so far in the story? (*Rosie, Lou the Lizard, Rosie's mom*)

   Why is Rosie's mom angry? (*Rosie didn't pick up her room.*)

   Rosie has a problem. What is it? (*She isn't following directions.*)

   What does Rosie have to do before she can run in the big race? (*Follow her mom's directions to clean her room.*)

   Who does Rosie think can help her? (*Lou*)

3. Ask the children what they think the skill of Following Directions means. Praise them generously for their ideas. As much as possible, tie their ideas to the following definition.

> **Following Directions means that you listen, understand, and do what someone has asked you to do.**

If appropriate, direct the children's attention to the Following Directions poster. Leave the poster up for future reference.

4. Explain that children can use the skill of Following Directions right now, in their daily lives, and that they will continue to use it when they grow up. Ask them if they can think of situations where they could use the skill of Following Directions. Examples:

- Your teacher wants you to make something for art.

- Your mom or dad asks you to clean your room.

- You are trying to build a model.

- You have a fire drill.

Verbally reinforce children's responses and, if appropriate, write their ideas on an easel pad or dry erase board. Let them know that usually, they will follow instructions adults give them, but that sometimes, they may follow directions other children give (for instance, when a friend or classmate gives instructions for playing a game).

5. Share an example of Following Directions from your own life. For instance, you might say that you follow directions when you come to a stop sign to stay safe when you are driving.

6. Ask students why they think they should learn and use this skill. Discuss different possible reasons. Examples:

- You'll feel good.

- It will make you happy.

- You'll get things right the first time.

- Friends will want to include you in projects and activities.

- Parents will be happy because you are acting more responsibly.

- Teachers will be happy because you are ready and willing to learn.

Praise the children for their suggestions. Record the reasons on an easel pad or dry erase board, if you wish.

7. Give the following general rationale for using the skill of Following Directions:

It is important to follow directions to show that you are responsible and to learn new things.

CLOSING

1. Let students know that today they met three characters, Rosie, Rosie's mom, and Lou. They also learned the meaning of Following Directions and talked about some reasons the skill is important.

2. Distribute crayons or markers and give students time to color pages 1 and 2 in their Rosie the Roadrunner coloring books. As they color, assess their understanding of story content and lesson concepts. Ask:

Who is the roadrunner? What is her name? *(Rosie)*

What is Rosie's problem? *(She isn't following directions.)*

What does it mean to follow directions? *(Reinforce any part of the definition.)*

Why is it important to follow directions? *(to show you're responsible, to be able to learn)*

L E S S O N 2

In Lesson 1, children met Rosie, Rosie's mom, and Lou the Lizard and learned the definition of Following Directions.

In this lesson, children learn about the mnemonic **BEST.**

In Lesson 3, children will learn that the *B* in **BEST** tells you to keep your body straight, hands on your lap, and feet on the floor.

TEACHING GUIDE

For this lesson, you will need a CD player, the music CD, and puppets for the Rosie, Lou, and Sammy characters.

1. Remind students of what was happening in the story when you left off: Rosie was headed to see her friend Lou the Lizard, who could help her with her problem. Read pages 12–15 in the storybook.

2. Review this part of the story for students' comprehension, using the felt board and cutouts. Ask:

   Who is Lou? *(a lizard, Rosie's friend)*

   What is Lou going to teach Rosie? *(how to follow directions)*

   Lou said there were four steps in Following Directions. What did he call these? *(BEST)*

3. Tell students that **BEST** represents the four steps of the skill:

   | B | **Body** straight, hands on your lap, and feet on the floor. |

   | E | **Eyes** on the speaker. |

   | S | **Serious** face. |

   | T | **Turn** your body toward the speaker. |

If appropriate for your group, direct students' attention to the **BEST** skill poster. For younger children, use the felt board and letter cutouts and go over each step verbally.

4. Use the **BEST** song to verbally rehearse the skill steps. To do so:

- Read the lyrics on page 41 to the students aloud.

- Have students repeat the lyrics one or two times.

- Play the song.

- Choose the appropriate puppet as each character is mentioned in the song (Rosie, Lou, and Sammy) and pretend the puppet is doing the singing.

- Have the students sing along with the recording.

While singing the song, you could also model the steps as they are introduced: Stand or sit straight, point to your eyes and to the children's eyes, point to your face, and then turn toward the music.

5. Tell students that **BEST** represents the *nonverbal*, or nonspeaking, steps of the skill: You don't have to say anything to do these steps. Explain that the other part of Following Directions is the *doing* part of the skill: You go ahead and do what it is that you've been asked to do.

Repeat the idea that we follow directions from people we know and trust, not from strangers or from people who tell us to do something we know is wrong.

CLOSING

1. Review what the children learned today: There are four steps in the nonverbal part of the skill of Following Directions, and these skills are called **BEST**.

2. Give students markers or crayons and have them color page 3 in their Rosie the Roadrunner coloring books. Assess the children's understanding of the story content and lesson concepts while they color. Ask:

Who is Lou? *(a lizard, Rosie's friend)*

What is he teaching Rosie? *(how to follow directions)*

Lou said there were four steps in Following Directions. What did Lou call these four steps? *(BEST)*

L E S S O N   3

In Lesson 2, children learned that **BEST** stands for the nonverbal part of Following Directions.

In this lesson, children learn that the *B* in **BEST** tells you to keep your body straight, hands in your lap, and feet on the floor.

In Lesson 4, children will learn that the *E* in **BEST** tells you to keep your eyes on the speaker.

TEACHING GUIDE

1. Remind students of what was happening in the story when you left off: Lou told Rosie that there are four **BEST** behaviors. Read pages 16–23 in the storybook.

2. Review the story for comprehension, using the felt board and cutouts. Ask:

   What is Rosie's problem? *(She doesn't know how to follow directions.)*

   Lou said there were four steps in Following Directions. What did Lou call these steps? *(BEST)*

   What part of **BEST** is Lou teaching Rosie? *(how to keep her body straight, hands on her lap, and feet on the floor)*

   What does Rosie do after Lou teaches her this step? *(She runs home.)*

   What does Rosie's mom say to her when Rosie runs back home? *(Rosie isn't ready to race yet.)* Why?

3. Introduce the first step. Say:

   The first step in Following Directions is *B.* What does the *B* tell you to do when following directions? *(Keep your body straight, hands on your lap, and feet on the floor.)*

4. Give a rationale for using the *B* step. Say:

   The *B* in **BEST** tells you to keep your body straight, hands on your lap, and your feet on the floor. It is important to control your body when following directions so you don't distract the person giving the directions, others who may be listening, or yourself.

5. Demonstrate the *B* step in the following way. For this skill, you will need a partner, ideally another adult.

Model the Skill Step

In this and following role plays, you may model the step or steps either correctly or incorrectly at any time. If you model a step incorrectly, be sure to follow up with a correct one. (Students with cognitive disabilities may need to see correct modeling displays only.)

Choose a situation that requires skill use and describe it to students. For example, you could sit in a chair and say:

Let's pretend that _____ is my friend. _____ will tell me about a picnic we're going to have next week.

Have the other person begin telling you all the things you should bring (ketchup, napkins, chips, etc.). Model the *B* step.

Students Evaluate Modeling

Ask students the following questions:

Did I do the step correctly?

Did I do the step incorrectly?

If you did the step incorrectly, model it again correctly.

Students Verbally Rehearse the Skill Step

Have students use verbal rehearsal to memorize the *B* step:

B—Body straight, hands on your lap, and feet on the floor.

Students Practice the Skill Step

Invite students to describe a situation in which they can practice the *B* step. You could also use a situation you have observed recently or select one from the list of suggested role-play situations on page 39. Ask for volunteers to role-play the skill step.

Students Perform a Self-Check

After each role-play example, invite the children to evaluate performance of the *B* step:

What was good about this example?

What needs improvement?

CLOSING

1. Tell the students they now know that the *B* in **BEST** tells you to keep your body straight, hands on your lap, and feet on the floor.

2. Give students crayons or markers and have them color pages 4 and 5 in their Rosie the Roadrunner coloring books. Assess the children's understanding of the lesson concepts while they color. Ask:

   What are the four steps in Following Directions called?

   When you are following directions, what does the *B* in **BEST** tell you to do?

L E S S O N 4

In Lesson 3, children learned that the *B* in **BEST** tells you to keep your body straight, hands on your lap, and feet on the floor.

In this lesson, children learn that the *E* in **BEST** tells you to keep your eyes on the speaker.

In Lesson 5, children will learn that the *S* in **BEST** tells you to have a serious face.

TEACHING GUIDE

1. Remind students of what was happening in the story when you left off: Rosie tries out the *B* step, but her mom says she's not ready to race yet. She goes back to Lou for more advice. Read pages 24–31 in the storybook.

2. Review the story for comprehension, using the felt board and cutouts. Ask:

    What is Rosie learning to do? *(follow directions)*

    Lou said there were four steps in Following Directions. What did Lou call these? *(BEST)*

    The first step in **BEST** starts with the letter *B*. What does the *B* tell you to do with your body when following directions? *(Keep your body straight, hands on your lap, and feet on the floor.)*

    Today in the story, Lou showed Rosie what the *E* in **BEST** means. What does the *E* in **BEST** tell you to do when following directions? *(Keep your eyes on the speaker.)*

3. Give rationales for using the *B* and *E* steps. Say:

    The *B* in **BEST** tells you to keep your body straight, hands on your lap, and feet on the floor. It is important to control your body when following directions so you don't distract the person giving the directions, others who may be listening, or yourself.

    The *E* in **BEST** tells you to keep your eyes on the speaker. It is important to keep your eyes on the speaker because it shows the speaker that you care and are listening.

4. With a partner, demonstrate the *B* and *E* steps in the following way.

Model the Skill Steps

Continue with the situation you chose in Lesson 3. Have the other person tell you again all the things you should bring to the picnic (ketchup, napkins, chips, etc.). Model the *B* and *E* steps.

Students Evaluate Modeling

Ask students the following questions:

Did I do the steps correctly?

Did I do any steps incorrectly?

If you did any of the steps incorrectly, use another situation to model the steps correctly.

Students Verbally Rehearse the Skill Steps

Ask students to use verbal rehearsal to memorize the *B* and *E* steps:

B—Body straight, hands on your lap, and feet on the floor.

E—Eyes on the speaker.

Students Practice the Skill Steps

Invite students to generate a situation in which they can practice the *B* and *E* steps, use a situation you have observed recently, or select an example from the list of suggested role-play situations on page 39. Ask for volunteers to role-play the skill steps.

Students Perform a Self-Check

After each role-play example, invite the children to evaluate performance of the *B* and *E* steps. Ask:

What was good about this example?

What needs improvement?

CLOSING

1. Tell the students that they now know that the *B* in **BEST** tells you to keep your body straight, hands on your lap, and feet on the floor. They just learned that the *E* in **BEST** tells you to keep your eyes on the speaker.

2. Give students crayons or markers and have them color pages 6 and 7 in their Rosie the Roadrunner coloring books. Assess the children's understanding of story content and the lesson concepts while they color. Ask:

   When you are following directions, what does the *B* in **BEST** tell you to do?

   What does the *E* in **BEST** tell you to do?

L E S S O N   5

<table>
<tr>
<td>In Lesson 4, children learned that the *E* in **BEST** tells you to keep your eyes on the speaker.</td>
<td>In this lesson, children learn that the *S* in **BEST** tells you to have a serious face.</td>
<td>In Lesson 6, children will learn that the *T* in **BEST** tells you to turn your body toward the speaker.</td>
</tr>
</table>

TEACHING GUIDE

1. Remind students of what was happening in the story when you left off: Rosie "raps" (tells) what to do (the *B* and *E* steps). Read pages 32–37 in the storybook.

2. Review the story for comprehension, using the felt board and cutouts. Ask:

   Lou told Rosie there were four steps in Following Directions. What did Lou call these? *(BEST)*

   What does the *B* in **BEST** tell you to do when following directions? *(Keep your body straight, hands on your lap, and feet on the floor.)*

   What does the *E* in **BEST** tell you to do when following directions? *(Keep your eyes on the speaker.)*

   Today, Lou showed Rosie what the *S* in **BEST** means. What does the *S* in **BEST** tell you to do when following directions? *(Have a serious face.)*

   What does a serious face look like? *(Ask the children to show you.)*

3. Give the rationales for using the *B, E,* and *S* steps in **BEST.** Say:

   The *B* in **BEST** tells you to keep your body straight, hands on your lap, and feet on the floor. It is important to control your body when following directions so you don't distract the person giving the directions, others who may be listening, or yourself.

The *E* in **BEST** tells you to keep your eyes on the speaker. It is important to keep your eyes on the speaker because it shows you care and tells the speaker you are listening.

The *S* in **BEST** tells you to have a serious face. It is important to have a serious face because this helps keep you calm and shows the speaker that you want to understand what you should do.

If you wish, add: "Sometimes you might have a serious face and nod your head to let the person know you understand."

4. With a partner, demonstrate the *B*, *E*, and *S* steps in the following way.

Model the Skill Steps

Continue with the situation you began in Lesson 3. Have the other person tell you again all the things you should bring to the picnic (ketchup, napkins, chips, etc.). Model the *B*, *E*, and *S* steps.

Students Evaluate Modeling

Ask students:

Did I do the steps correctly?

Did I do any steps incorrectly?

If you did any of the steps incorrectly, model the steps again correctly.

Students Verbally Rehearse the Skill Steps

Have students use verbal rehearsal to memorize the *B*, *E*, and *S* steps:

B—Body straight, hands on your lap, and feet on the floor.

E—Eyes on the speaker.

S—Serious face.

Students Practice the Skill Steps

Invite students to generate a situation in which they can practice the *B*, *E*, and *S* steps, use a situation you have observed recently, or select one from the list of suggested role-play situations on page 39. Ask for volunteers to role-play the skill steps.

Students Perform a Self-Check

After each role-play example, invite the children to evaluate performance of the *B*, *E*, and *S* steps. Ask:

What was good about this example?

What needs improvement?

CLOSING

1. Tell students that they now know that the *B* in **BEST** tells you to keep your body straight, hands on your lap, and feet on the floor and that the *E* in **BEST** tells you to keep your eyes on the speaker. They just learned that the *S* in **BEST** tells you to have a serious face.

2. Give students crayons or markers and have them color pages 8 and 9 in their Rosie the Roadrunner coloring books. Assess the children's understanding of story content and lesson concepts while they color. Ask:

When you are following directions, what does the *B* in **BEST** tell you to do?

What does the *E* in **BEST** tell you to do?

What does the *S* in **BEST** tell you to do?

L E S S O N 6

In Lesson 5, children learned that the *S* in **BEST** tells you to have a serious face.

In this lesson, children learn that the *T* in **BEST** tells you to turn your body toward the speaker.

In Lesson 7, children will practice **BEST** and learn to identify the *doing* part of Following Directions.

TEACHING GUIDE

1. Remind students of what was happening in the story when you left off: Rosie had learned to keep a serious face and said she was ready to show her mom what she had learned. Read pages 38–43 in the storybook.

2. Review this part of the story for comprehension, using the felt board and cutouts. Ask:

   Lou told Rosie there were four steps in Following Directions. What did Lou call these? *(BEST)*

   What does the *B* in **BEST** tell you to do when following directions? *(Keep your body straight, hands on your lap, and feet on the floor.)*

   What does the *E* in **BEST** tell you to do when following directions? *(Keep your eyes on the speaker.)*

   What does the *S* in **BEST** tell you to do when following directions? *(Have a serious face.)*

   Today, Lou told Rosie what the *T* in **BEST** tells you to do when following directions. What does *T* mean? *(Turn your body toward the speaker.)*

3. Give rationales for the *B, E, S,* and *T* steps in **BEST**.

   The *B* in **BEST** tells you to keep your body straight, hands on your lap, and feet on the floor when following directions. It is important to control your body when following directions so you don't distract the person giving the directions, others who may be listening, or yourself.

The *E* tells you to keep your eyes on the speaker. It is important to keep your eyes on the speaker because it shows you care and tells the speaker you are listening.

The *S* tells you to have a serious face. It is important to have a serious face because this helps keep you calm and shows the speaker that you want to understand what you should do.

The *T* tells you to turn your body toward the speaker. It is important to turn your body toward the speaker when following directions to show that you are giving the speaker your full attention.

4. With a partner, demonstrate the *B, E, S,* and *T* steps in the following way.

Model the Skill Steps

Continue with the situation you began in Lesson 3. Have the other person tell you all the things you should bring (ketchup, napkins, chips, etc.). Model the *B, E, S,* and *T* steps.

Students Evaluate Modeling

Ask students:

Did I do the steps correctly?

Did I do any steps incorrectly?

If you did any of the steps incorrectly, model the steps again correctly.

Students Verbally Rehearse the Skill Steps

Have students use verbal rehearsal to memorize the *B, E, S,* and *T* steps:

B—**Body** straight, hands on your lap, and feet on the floor.

E—**Eyes** on the speaker.

S—**Serious** face.

T—**Turn** your body toward the speaker.

Students Practice the Skill Steps

Invite students to generate a situation in which they can practice the *B*, *E*, *S*, and *T* steps, use a situation you have observed recently, or select one from the list of suggested role-play situations on page 39. Ask for volunteers to role-play the skill steps.

Students Perform a Self-Check

After each role-play example, invite the children to evaluate performance of the *B*, *E*, *S*, and *T* steps. Ask:

What was good about this example?

What needs improvement?

CLOSING

1. Tell students they now know that the *B* in **BEST** tells you to keep your body straight, hands on your lap, and feet on the floor. They also know that the *E* in **BEST** tells you to keep your eyes on the speaker and that the *S* in **BEST** tells you to have a serious face when following directions. They just learned that the *T* in **BEST** means that you turn your body toward the speaker.

2. Give students crayons or markers and have them color page 10 in their Rosie the Roadrunner coloring book. Assess their understanding of story content and lesson concepts while they color. Ask:

When you are following directions, what does the *B* in **BEST** tell you to do?

What does the *E* in **BEST** tell you to do?

What does the *S* in **BEST** tell you to do?

What does the *T* in **BEST** tell you to do?

In Lesson 6, children learned the *T* step in **BEST.**

In this lesson, children learn about the *doing* part of the Following Directions skill.

TEACHING GUIDE

For this lesson, you'll need an assortment of picnic items and a bag to put them in.

1. Remind students of what was happening in the story when you left off: Rosie had learned the *T* step and was ready to go home and do the skill alone. Read pages 44–53 in the storybook.

2. Review this part of the story for students' comprehension, using the felt board and cutouts. Ask:

   When Rosie followed directions, she did her very _____ . *(BEST)*

   What did Rosie do for her mom? *(Rosie cleaned up her room.)*

   Mom let Rosie go to the big, big _____ . *(race)*

   And who won the race that day? Who was the fastest? *(Rosie)*

   What did Rosie win? *(desert running shoes)*

3. Review the rationales for the *B, E, S,* and *T* steps in **BEST.** Say:

   The *B* in **BEST** tells you to keep your body straight, hands on your lap, and feet on the floor when following directions. It is important to control your body when following directions so you don't distract the person giving the directions, others who may be listening, or yourself.

   The *E* tells you to keep your eyes on the speaker. It is important to keep your eyes on the speaker because it shows you care and tells the speaker you are listening.

   The *S* tells you to have a serious face. It is important to have a serious face because this helps keep you calm and shows the speaker that you want to understand what you should do.

The *T* tells you to turn your body toward the speaker. It is important to turn your body toward the speaker when following directions to show that you are giving the speaker your full attention.

4. Remind students that **BEST** is the *nonverbal* part of Following Directions—in other words, the part you can do without saying anything. Explain that the second part of the skill is the *doing* part—you go ahead and do what you have been asked to do.

5. With a partner, demonstrate the *B, E, S,* and *T* steps.

Model the Skill Steps

Continue with the situation you began in Lesson 3. Have the other person tell you again all the things you should bring to the picnic (ketchup, napkins, chips, etc.). Model the *B, E, S,* and *T* steps. This time, gather up all the picnic items, put them in the bag, and pretend to take them away with you to the picnic.

Students Evaluate Modeling

Ask students:

Did I do the steps correctly?

Did I do any steps incorrectly?

If you did any of the steps incorrectly, model them again correctly.

Students Verbally Rehearse the Skill Steps

Have students use verbal rehearsal to memorize the *B, E, S,* and *T* steps:

B—Body straight, hands on your lap, and feet on the floor.

E—Eyes on the speaker.

S—Serious face.

T—Turn your body toward the speaker.

Also have students verbally rehearse the *doing* part of the skill step:

Do what you have been asked to do.

Students Practice the Skill Steps

Invite students to generate a situation in which they can practice the *B*, *E*, *S*, and *T* steps, use a situation you have observed recently, or choose an example from the suggested role-play situations on page 39. Ask for volunteers to role-play the skill steps. Be sure they add the *doing* component of the skill.

Students Perform a Self-Check

After each role-play example, invite the children to evaluate performance of the *B*, *E*, *S*, and *T* steps. Ask:

What was good about this example?

What needs improvement?

Also ask:

Did _____ follow directions? Did he or she do what the speaker asked?

CLOSING

1. Tell students they have done a great job learning how to do their **BEST** to follow directions. They know that Rosie did her **BEST** to follow directions by *B* (keeping her body straight, hands on her lap, and feet on the floor), *E* (keeping her eyes on the speaker), *S* (having a serious face), and *T* (turning her body toward the speaker).

   They also learned that Rosie followed directions by doing what her mom asked her to do *(clean up her room)*. She won the big race and got some cool desert running shoes.

2. Give students the crayons or markers and have them color pages 11 and 12 in their Rosie the Roadrunner coloring books. Assess their understanding of story content and lesson concepts while they color. Ask:

   When you follow directions, what does the *B* in **BEST** tell you to do?

   What does the *E* in **BEST** tell you to do?

   What does the *S* in **BEST** tell you to do?

   What does the *T* in **BEST** tell you to do?

   What else do you have to do when you are asked to follow directions? *(Go ahead and do what you have been asked to do.)*

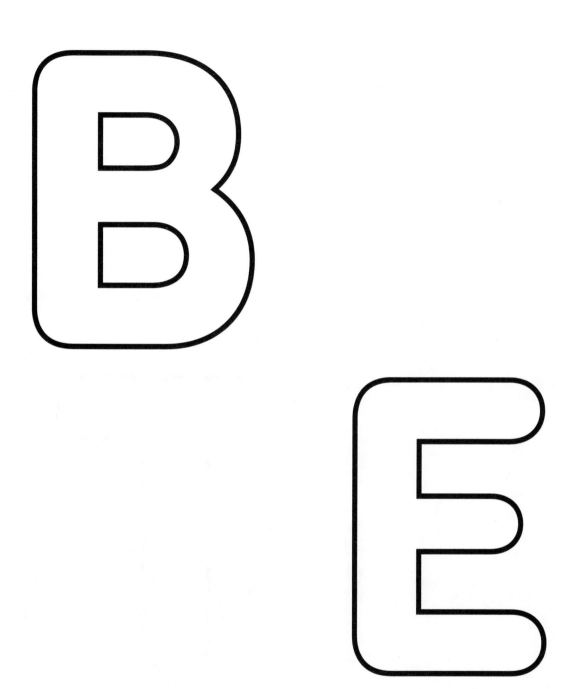

Felt Board Patterns (cont.)

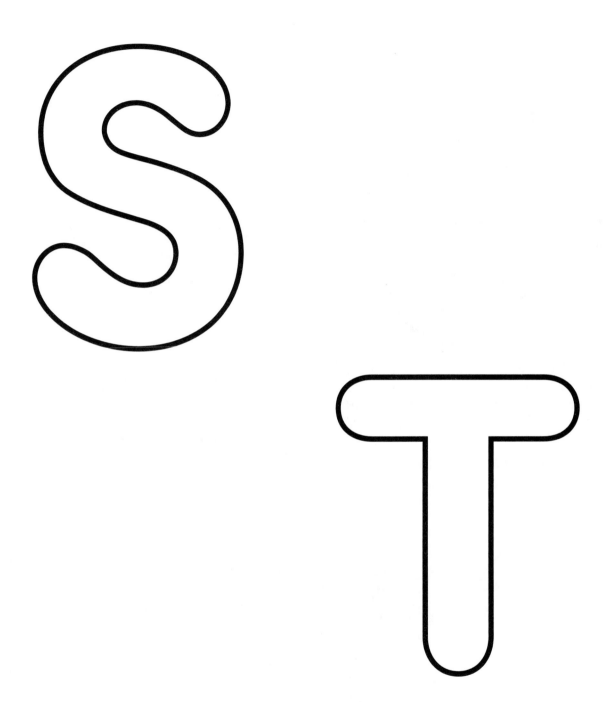

Rosie the Roadrunner

From *Social Skills in Pictures, Stories, and Songs,* by L. A. Serna, M. E. Nielsen, and S. R. Forness, © 2007, Champaign, IL: Research Press (www.researchpress.com; 800–519–2707).

Lou the Lizard

Rosie's Mom

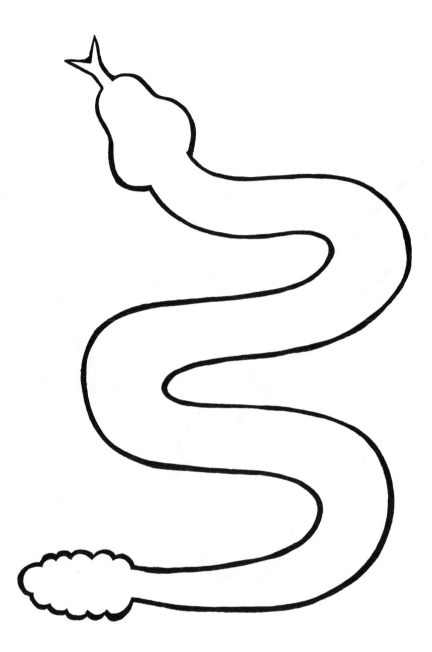

Sammy the Snake

From *Social Skills in Pictures, Stories, and Songs,* by L. A. Serna, M. E. Nielsen, and S. R. Forness, © 2007, Champaign, IL: Research Press (www.researchpress.com; 800–519–2707).

Following Directions

Following Directions means that you listen, understand, and do what someone has asked you to do.

From *Social Skills in Pictures, Stories, and Songs*, by L. A. Serna, M. E. Nielsen, and S. R. Forness, © 2007, Champaign, IL: Research Press (www.researchpress.com; 800–519–2707).

Following Directions

B **Body** straight, hands on your lap, and feet on the floor.

E **Eyes** on the speaker.

S **Serious** face.

T **Turn** your body toward the speaker.

From *Social Skills in Pictures, Stories, and Songs,* by L. A. Serna, M. E. Nielsen, and S. R. Forness, © 2007, Champaign, IL: Research Press (www.researchpress.com; 800–519–2707).

Suggested Role-Play Situations: Following Directions

1. Let's pretend that your class is getting ready to go outside to recess. I'll be the teacher, and let's act out the situation. I'll say, "_____, please line up at the door."

    • What should you do?

    • Show me.

2. I'll be your parent. Let's pretend we are in the kitchen. I'll say, "_____ , please put the milk in the refrigerator."

    • What should you do?

    • Show me.

3. Let's pretend that we are getting ready to have dinner. I'll be your parent. I'll say, "_____ , would you go wash your hands?"

    • What should you do?

    • Show me.

4. Pretend we are in the classroom. I'll be your teacher. I'll say, "Please raise your hand if you know what the weather is like outside."

    • What should you do?

    • Show me.

5. Your teacher just passed out a piece of paper. Pretend I am your teacher. I'll say, "Class, please get out a red crayon and draw a picture of _____ ."

    • What should you do?

    • Show me.

From *Social Skills in Pictures, Stories, and Songs,* by L. A. Serna, M. E. Nielsen, and S. R. Forness, © 2007, Champaign, IL: Research Press (www.researchpress.com; 800–519–2707).

Song Sheet
BEST: Rosie the Roadrunner Learns to Follow Directions

Music and lyrics by L. Dennis Higgins

Lyrics
BEST: Rosie the Roadrunner Learns to Follow Directions

Music and lyrics by L. Dennis Higgins

Please listen, and just try your **BEST.**

I have a friend, Lou is his name,
he's a spotted lizard from the Southwest.
He taught me this song—I'll teach it to you.

Please listen, and just try your **BEST.**

My body is straight,
my eyes are on you.
I have a serious face,
not a frown, not a frown, not a frown,
   not a frown.

My hands are in my lap,
my feet are on the ground,
I'll turn my body, but I won't turn around.

Please listen, and just try your **BEST.**

I have a friend, Rosie is her name,
she's a roadrunner from the Southwest.
She taught me this song—I'll teach it to you.

Please listen, and just try your **BEST.**

My body is straight,
my eyes are on you.
I have a serious face,
not a frown, not a frown, not a frown,
   not a frown.

My hands are in my lap,
my feet are on the ground,
I'll turn my body, but I won't turn around.

Please listen, and just try your **BEST.**

I have a friend, Sammy is his name,
he's a rattlesnake from the Southwest.
He taught me this song—I'll teach it to you.

Please listen, and just try your **BEST.**

My body is straight,
my eyes are on you.
I have a serious face,
not a frown, not a frown, not a frown,
   not a frown.

My hands are in my lap,
my feet are on the ground,
I'll turn my body, but I won't turn around.
I'll turn my body, but I won't turn around . . .

From *Social Skills in Pictures, Stories, and Songs,* by L. A. Serna, M. E. Nielsen, and S. R. Forness, © 2007, Champaign, IL: Research Press (www.researchpress.com; 800–519–2707).

Sharing

Prairie Dog Pete

SKILL DEFINITION

Sharing means letting someone take something you have
or letting someone use something after you've finished with it.

SKILL STEPS

| P | Put your **BEST** behaviors forward. |

| A | Ask yourself, "Is there enough to share?" |

| L | Let someone know if you'll share, yes or no. |

| S | Share now or share later. |

NOTE

There are some situations in which sharing may not be appropriate—for instance, one's coat when it's cold out, all of one's lunch, or one's only pencil. This skill applies to situations in which children can reasonably be expected to share.

L E S S O N   1

In this lesson, children meet Prairie Dog Pete and Sally O'Shay and learn the definition of Sharing.

In Lesson 2, children learn about the mnemonic **PALS**.

TEACHING GUIDE

Introduce the skill by letting students know that today they will begin learning about Prairie Dog Pete and the skill of Sharing.

1. Read pages 55–65 of the storybook.

2. Review this part of the story for comprehension, using the felt board and cutouts. Ask:

    Who are the characters so far in the story? *(Prairie Dog Pete and Sally O'Shay)*

    Where does Pete live? *(on the flatlands, in a burrow, underground)*

    What does Pete have lots and lots of? *(toys)*

    What is Pete's problem? *(He does not want to share.)*

    How does Sally feel when Pete won't share with her? *(sad, disappointed)*

    What kind of contest are the prairie dogs planning? *(a digging contest)*

3. Ask the children what they think the skill of Sharing means. Praise the children generously for their suggestions. As much as possible, tie their ideas to the following definition.

> **Sharing means letting someone take something you have or letting someone use something after you've finished with it.**

If appropriate, direct the children's attention to the Sharing definition poster. Leave the poster up for future reference.

4. Explain that Sharing is a skill that the children can use right now when they are at home or school, or in other places. The skill will

also help them as they grow up. Get students' ideas about different situations that require use of the skill. Examples:

- You are riding a bicycle on the playground, and someone else wants to ride it.

- You are playing with blocks, and someone asks if he or she can play with you.

- You are on the computer, and someone else wants to use it, too.

- You are at home playing with your toys, and your brother or sister wants to play with you.

- You are having lunch and serving yourself your favorite food, and others want some, too.

Verbally reinforce students' contributions. If you wish, record the examples on an easel pad or dry erase board.

5. Give a personal example of sharing from your own life. For example, you might say that you use the skill of Sharing when you order pizza for your family. When you serve yourself, you make sure to leave enough slices for the other people in your family.

6. Discuss the different reasons for using the skill of Sharing. Ask the students why they think this skill is important, and praise them for their suggestions. For example:

- Sharing makes you happy.

- It feels good to be nice to others.

- Others will want to play with you because you are nice and willing to be a friend and share.

- Parents and teachers will be happy because you are getting along with others and sharing your things.

- If you share, you will have many friends who like being with you because you are nice.

- If you share, the person you share with will be more likely to share with you.

7. Give a general rationale for the skill of sharing:

It is important to share with others to show others that you care and want to be a good friend or family member.

CLOSING

1. Tell the students that they have now met Prairie Dog Pete and Sally O'Shay. They have also talked about the meaning of Sharing. They have also discussed times they could use the skill and reasons for using it.

2. Provide crayons or markers and give students time to color pages 1–4 in their Prairie Dog Pete coloring books. Assess the children's understanding of story content and lesson concepts while they are coloring. Ask:

   What is the main character's name? *(Prairie Dog Pete)*

   Who is his friend? *(Sally O'Shay)*

   Pete has a problem. What is it? *(He doesn't want to share.)*

   What did Pete say about his toys? *(They're all mine, mine, mine, mine.)*

   What does Sharing mean? *(Accept any part of the definition, then review the entire definition.)*

L E S S O N   2

In Lesson 1, children met Prairie Dog Pete and Sally O'Shay and learned the definition of Sharing.

In this lesson, children are introduced to the mnemonic **PALS** and learn that the *P* step means to put your **BEST** behaviors forward.

In Lesson 3, children will learn that in **PALS**, the *A* step tells you to ask yourself if you can share, and the *L* step tells you to let the other person know if you'll share—yes or no.

TEACHING GUIDE

For this lesson, you will need a CD player, the music CD, and puppets for the Pete, Sally, and Jack characters.

1. Remind students of what was happening in the story when you left off: Sally felt disappointed that Pete wouldn't share with her and was telling the other prairie dogs that it wasn't fair. Read pages 66–73 in the storybook.

2. Review this part of the story for comprehension, using the felt board and cutouts. Ask:

   Who is this? *(Point to the Pete cutout.)*

   Who is this? *(Point to the Sally cutout.)*

   Who is this? *(Point to the Jack the Jack Rabbit cutout.)*

   What is Jack going to teach Pete? *(how to share)*

3. Say: "Jack said there were four steps to sharing. What did he call these steps?" *(PALS)*

   Let students know that PALS represents the four steps of the skill:

P	**Put** your **BEST** behaviors forward.
A	**Ask** yourself, "Is there enough to share?"

| L | **Let** someone know if you'll share, yes or no. |

| S | **Share** now or share later. |

If appropriate for your group, direct students' attention to the PALS skill poster. For younger children, use the felt board and letter cutouts and go over each step verbally.

4. Use the **PALS** song to verbally rehearse the skill steps. To do so:

   Read the lyrics on page 69 aloud.

   Have students repeat the lyrics one or two times.

   Play the song.

   Choose the appropriate puppet as each character is mentioned in the song (Pete, Sally, and Jack) and pretend the puppet is doing the singing.

   Have the students sing along with the recording.

5. Ask: "Why do you think we use the word *PALS* to help us remember to share? (*PALS helps us remember the steps in the skill.*)

6. Introduce and discuss the *P* step in **PALS**. Say:

   The *P* in **PALS** tells you to put your **BEST** behaviors forward. It's as easy as can be. You know to use body posture (*B*) and good eye contact (*E*) to let others know you're listening. And you also have to keep a serious (*S*) face to show you're aware, and then turn (*T*) toward the other person to show you're ready to share.

7. Give a rationale for using the *P* step. Say:

   The *P* step in **PALS** tells you to put your **BEST** behaviors forward. This step is important because it shows the other person that you are ready to share.

8. With another person (ideally another adult), demonstrate the skill step in the following way.

Model the Skill Step

In this and following role plays, you may model the step or steps either correctly or incorrectly at any time. If you model a step incorrectly, be sure to follow up with a correct one. (Students with cognitive disabilities may need to see correct modeling displays only.)

Choose a situation that requires skill use and describe it to students. For example, you could say:

> Let's suppose that _____ is walking to school with me, and I have a package of _____'s favorite candy.

Have the other person say your name. Model the *P* in **PALS** by demonstrating the **BEST** behaviors. Reply, "Yes?"

Students Evaluate Modeling

Ask students the following questions:

> Did I do this step correctly?
>
> Did I do this step incorrectly?

If you did the step incorrectly, model it again, this time correctly.

Students Verbally Rehearse the Skill Step

Have students use verbal rehearsal to memorize the *P* step:

> **P—Put** your **BEST** behavior forward.

Students Practice the Skill Step

Ask students to describe a situation in which they can use the *P* step. You may also use a situation you have observed recently or select one from the list of suggested role-play situations on page XX. Ask for volunteers to role-play the step.

Students Perform a Self-Check

After each example, invite the children to evaluate performance of the *P* step. Ask:

> What was good about this example?
>
> What needs improvement?

CLOSING

1. Tell the students that they now know that the *P* in **PALS** tells you to put your **BEST** behaviors forward. That means using good body posture and eye contact, keeping a serious face, and turning toward the other person to show you're ready to share.

2. Provide crayons or markers and have the children color pages 5–7 in their Prairie Dog Pete coloring books. Assess the children's understanding of story content and lesson concepts while they color. Ask:

   Who is this? *(Point to Jack the Jack Rabbit.)*

   What is Jack teaching Pete? *(how to use PALS to share)*

   When you share with others, what does the *P* in **PALS** tell you to do? *(Put your BEST behaviors forward.)*

In Lesson 2, children were introduced to the mnemonic **PALS** and learned that the *P* in **PALS** tells you to put your **BEST** behaviors forward.

In this lesson, children learn that the *A* in **PALS** means ask yourself, "Can I share?" and that the *L* in **PALS** means to let someone know you'll share, yes or no.

In Lesson 4, children learn that the *S* in **PALS** means share now or share later.

TEACHING GUIDE

1. Remind students about what was happening in the story when you left off: Jack was helping Pete learn to share by telling him about **PALS.** Read pages 74–85 in the storybook.

2. Review this part of the story for comprehension, using the felt board and cutouts. Ask:

   What is Pete learning to do? *(share)*

   Jack said there were four steps to sharing. What did Jack call these steps? *(PALS)*

   The first step in **PALS** starts with the letter *P.* What does the *P* tell you to do when sharing? *(Put your BEST behaviors forward.)*

   Today, Pete learned that the *A* in **PALS** tells you to do what when sharing? *(Ask yourself, "Can I share?")*

3. Explain that when you ask yourself the question "Can I share?" you should ask yourself two additional questions. Say:

   Jack said the *A* in **PALS** also tells you to ask yourself, "Do I have enough to share?" After Jack tells him this, what does Pete say he will share and why? *(a bucket—because he has two of them)*

   What happens when Sally comes to ask Pete to share his new shovel? *(Pete says no.)*

   What else did Jack say the *A* tells you to ask yourself? *(How will sharing make me feel?)*

   How do you feel when you share something?

4. Say:

> Pete was busy learning many things today. Jack taught him what the *L* in **PALS** tells you to do when sharing. What does the *L* mean? *(Let someone know if you'll share, yes or no.)*

> If sharing right now is not something you can do, what can you tell someone? *(Tell the person that you will share later or that he or she will need to wait.)*

5. Give rationales for the *P*, *A*, and *L* steps:

> The *P* step tells you to put your **BEST** behaviors forward. This step is important to show that you are ready to share.

> The *A* step means ask yourself, "Can I share?" This step also tells you to ask yourself whether you have enough to share and how sharing will make you feel. Asking yourself these questions allows you to get all the facts before you make a decision to share.

> The *L* step means let someone know if you'll share, yes or no. This step is important because it lets the other person know your decision.

6. With a partner, model the *P*, *A*, and *L* steps in the following way.

Model the Skill Steps

> Continue with the situation you chose in Lesson 2. Model the *P*, *A*, and *L* steps. For example, you might say:

> Last time, I had a sharing situation. What was it? *(You were walking to school and had a package of your friend's favorite candy.)*

Have the other person say your name, then model the *P* in **PALS** by demonstrating the **BEST** behaviors. Have the other person ask you nicely to share.

Model the *A* step:

> So what do I need to do? *(Students respond.)* That's right—I need to ask myself, "Can I share?"

> What else do I have to ask myself? *(Students respond.)* I ask myself, "Do I have enough to share?" Well, yes, I have a whole box here.

> I also ask myself, "How will sharing make me feel?" I'll feel good if I share my candy with _____ . I know it's _____'s favorite."

Model the *L* step:

> What's next? *(Students respond.)* Very good! I need to let the other person know my decision.

Turn to your partner and say, "Yes. I'll share some candy with you."

Students Evaluate Modeling

Ask students the following questions:

Did I perform the steps correctly?

Did I perform any steps incorrectly?

If you modeled any of the steps incorrectly, model them again correctly.

Students Verbally Rehearse the Skill Steps

Ask students to use verbal rehearsal to memorize the *P*, *A*, and *L* steps:

P—**Put** your **BEST** behavior forward.

A—**Ask** yourself, "Can I share?"

L—**Let** someone know if you'll share.

Students Practice the Skill Steps

Invite students to generate a situation in which they can practice the *P*, *A*, and *L* steps; use a situation you have observed recently; or select one from the list of suggested role-play situations on page 67. Ask for volunteers to role-play the steps.

Students Perform a Self-Check

After each example, have children evaluate their performance of steps *P*, *A*, and *L*. Ask:

What was good about this example?

What needs improvement?

CLOSING

1. Tell the students that they now know that the *P* in **PALS** tells you to put your **BEST** behaviors forward when sharing. They just learned that the *A* in **PALS** tells you to ask yourself, "Can I share?"

They also learned that the *L* in **PALS** tells you to let someone know if you'll share, yes or no.

2. Provide crayons or markers and have the children color pages 8–10 of their Prairie Dog Pete coloring books. As they color, assess their understanding of story content and lesson concepts. Ask:

> When you share, what does the *P* in **PALS** tell you to do? (*Put your BEST behaviors forward.*)

> What does the *A* in **PALS** tell you to do? (*Ask yourself, "Can I share?" Also, "Is there enough to share?" and "How will sharing make me feel?"*)

> How do you think Pete will feel if he shares with Sally?

> What does the *L* tell you to do? (*Let the other person know, say yes or no.*)

L E S S O N   4

In Lesson 3, children learned that the *A* in **PALS** means ask yourself, "Can I share?" and that the *L* means let someone know you'll share, yes or no.

In this lesson, children will learn that the *S* in **PALS** means share now or share later.

TEACHING GUIDE

1. Remind students where you were in the story when you left off: Jack was telling Pete that he needs to use the *L* step in **PALS,** let the other person know whether you'll share, yes or no. Read pages 86–91 in the storybook.

2. Review this part of the story for comprehension, using the felt board and cutouts. Ask:

   What is Pete learning to do? *(Share).*

   Jack said there were four steps to sharing. What did Jack call these steps? *(PALS)*

   The first step in **PALS** starts with the letter *P.* What does the *P* tell you to do when sharing? *(Put your BEST behaviors forward.)*

   The second step in **PALS** is *A.* What does the *A* tell you to do when sharing? *(Ask yourself, "Can I share?" Also, "Do I have enough to share?" and "How would sharing make me feel?")*

   How does sharing make you feel? *(good, happy)*

   The third step in **PALS** is *L.* What does the *L* tell you to do when sharing? *(Let someone know if you'll share, yes or no.)*

   Today, Pete learned the fourth and final step in **PALS.** Jack said the *S* in **PALS** tells you to do what? *(Share now or share later, then you are done.)*

   Who won the digging contest? *(Sally and Pete)*

3. Give rationales for the *P*, *A*, *L*, and *S* steps.

> The *P* step tells you to put your **BEST** behaviors forward. This step is important to show that you are ready to share.

> The *A* step means ask yourself, "Can I share?" This step also tells you to ask yourself whether you have enough to share and how sharing will make you feel. Asking yourself these questions allows you to get all the facts before you make a decision to share.

> The *L* step means let someone know if you'll share, yes or no. This step is important because it lets the other person know your decision.

> The *S* step means share now or share later. This step is important because it helps you and the other person be happy, and you can feel good about yourself.

4. With a partner, demonstrate all of the skill steps together.

Model the Skill Steps

Continue with the situation you introduced in Lesson 2. Model the *P*, *A*, *L*, and *S* steps. For example, you could say:

> Who can tell me about the sharing situation we were working on last time? (*You were walking to school and your friend asked you to share your candy.*)

Model the *P*, *A*, and *L* steps as you did in Lesson 3. Add the *S* step:

> Will I share now or later?

Demonstrate sharing now by pretending to give your partner some candy. Or, if you wish, you could say, "We're already at school now, so I'll give you some at lunch, OK?"

Students Evaluate Modeling

Ask students the following questions:

> Did I do the steps correctly?

> Did I do any steps incorrectly?

If you did any of the steps incorrectly, model them again correctly.

Students Verbally Rehearse the Skill Steps

Have students use verbal rehearsal to memorize all the skill steps:

P—**Put** your **BEST** behaviors forward.

A—**Ask** yourself, "Is there enough to share?"

L—**Let** someone know if you'll share, yes or no.

S—**Share** now or share later.

Students Practice the Skill Steps

Invite students to generate a situation in which they can practice all the steps, use a situation you have observed recently, or select one from the list of suggested role-play situations on page 67. Ask for volunteers to role-play the steps.

Students Perform a Self-Check

After each role-play example, have children evaluate the performance of the entire **PALS** skill. Ask:

What was good about this example?

What needs improvement?

CLOSING

1. Tell the students that they now know that the *P* in **PALS** tells you to put your **BEST** behaviors forward; the *A* tells you to ask yourself, "Can I share?" The *L* tells you to let someone know if you'll share, yes or no. They just learned that the *S* tells you to share now or share later.

2. Provide crayons or markers and have the children color pages 11–12 in their Prairie Dog Pete coloring books. Assess the children's understanding of story content and lesson concepts while they color. Ask:

   When you are sharing, **PALS** spells what to do. When you share, what does the *P* in **PALS** tell you to do?

   What does the *A* in **PALS** tell you to do?

What does the *L* in **PALS** tell you to do?

What does the *S* in **PALS** tell you to do?

What did Sally and Pete do that helped them win the digging contest? *(They shared Pete's digging tools.)*

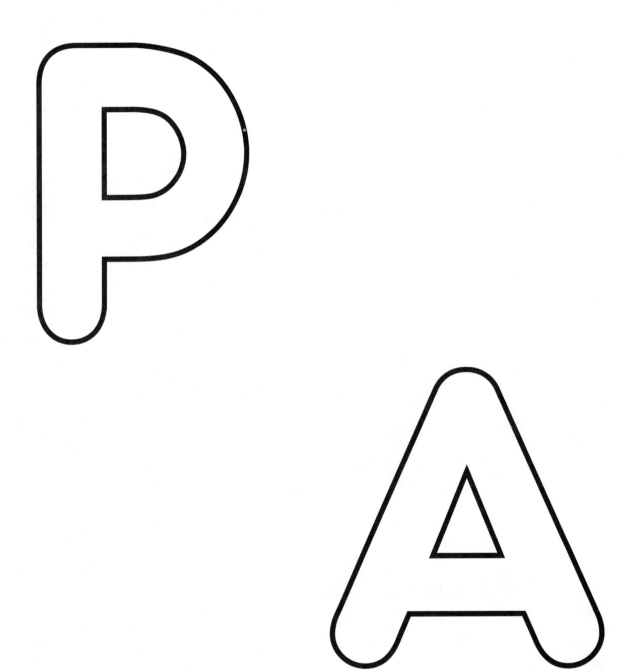

Felt Board Patterns (cont.)

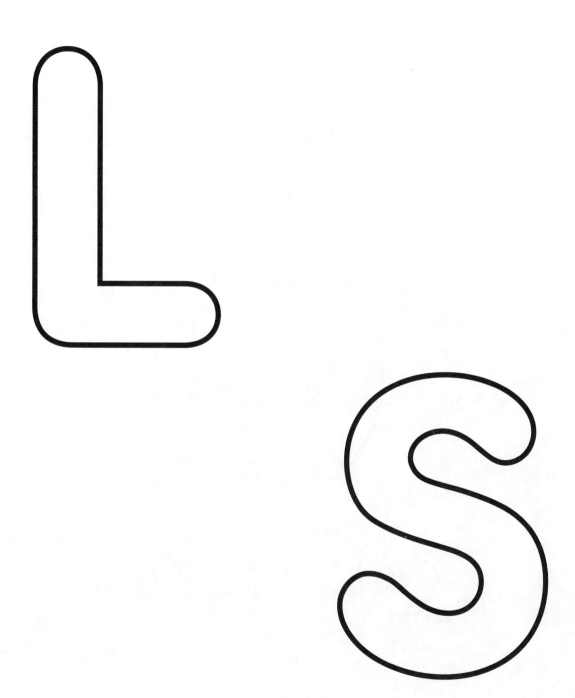

Prairie Dog Pete

Felt Board Patterns (cont.)

Sally O'Shay

Jack Rabbit Jack

Sharing

Sharing means letting someone take what you have or letting someone use something after you've finished with it.

From *Social Skills in Pictures, Stories, and Songs*, by L. A. Serna, M. E. Nielsen, and S. R. Forness, © 2007, Champaign, IL: Research Press (www.researchpress.com; 800–519–2707).

Sharing

P Put your **BEST** behaviors forward.

A Ask yourself, "Can I share?"

L Let someone know if you'll share, yes or no.

S Share now or share later.

From *Social Skills in Pictures, Stories, and Songs*, by L. A. Serna, M. E. Nielsen, and S. R. Forness, © 2007, Champaign, IL: Research Press (www.researchpress.com; 800–519–2707).

Suggested Role-Play Situations: Sharing

1. Pretend I am one of your friends and we are coloring a picture. I say, "_____ , can I borrow your brown crayon?"

   - What should you do?
   - Show me.

2. You are playing at one of the learning centers in your classroom. A friend comes up to you. I'll be that friend. I say, "Hi, _____ . Can I use one of your puzzles?"

   - What should you do?
   - Show me.

3. We are outside on the playground. I'll be one of your friends. I say, "Hey, _____ . Can I play with your ball?"

   - What should you do?
   - Show me.

4. You are eating lunch with your class. I'll be a friend who is sitting next to you. I say, "_____ , can I have some of your French fries?"

   - What should you do?
   - Show me.

5. You are at home, and I'll be your brother or sister. I say, "_____ , can I play with your game?"

   - What should you do?
   - Show me.

From *Social Skills in Pictures, Stories, and Songs,* by L. A. Serna, M. E. Nielsen, and S. R. Forness, © 2007, Champaign, IL: Research Press (www.researchpress.com; 800–519–2707).

Song Sheet
PALS: Prairie Dog Pete Learns to Share

Music and lyrics by L. Dennis Higgins

Lyrics
PALS: Prairie Dog Pete Learns to Share

Music and lyrics by L. Dennis Higgins

Prairie Dog Pete didn't know how to share.
Sally O'Shay said he wasn't playing fair.
Jack Rabbit Jack said, "Hip, hop, hello!"
But Prairie Dog Pete turned around and told him no.

It's not polite to say, "It's mine, mine, mine, mine, mine."
Two can share their things—it's fine, fine, fine, fine, fine.
It's easy to say, "I'd like to share with you."
So let's be **PALS**—that's all you have to do.

So let's be **PALS,**
you and me **PALS,**
we've got to be **PALS,**
I want to be **PALS.**

P—Put forth your **BEST** and show you care.
A—Ask yourself, "Can I share?"
L—Let someone know you'll share.
S—"Share! Yes, I will share."

Prairie Dog Pete didn't know how to share.
Jack Rabbit Jack said, "Hip, hop, hello!"
Sally O'Shay said he wasn't playing fair.
Jack Rabbit Jack said, "Hip, hop, hello!"

Managing Your Behavior

Roscoe the Raccoon

SKILL DEFINITION

Managing Your Behavior means that you try your BEST, evaluate yourself and adjust your behavior if you need to, and make sure to reward yourself.

SKILL STEPS

T   **Try** your **BEST.**

E   **Evaluate** yourself.

A   **Ask** yourself, "Am I doing my **BEST?**"

M   **Make** sure to reward yourself.

NOTE

It is helpful to let students know that they can use the skill of Managing Your Behavior both when they are in groups and when they are by themselves.

L E S S O N 1

In this lesson, students meet Roscoe the Raccoon and his family and learn the definition of Managing Your Behavior.

In Lesson 2, children learn about the mnemonic **TEAM.**

TEACHING GUIDE

Introduce the skill by letting students know that today they will begin learning about Roscoe the Raccoon and the skill of Managing Your Behavior.

1. Read pages 94–105 in the storybook.

2. Review this part of the story for comprehension, using the felt board and cutouts. Ask:

   Who are the characters in this story so far? *(Roscoe, Papa, Bandit, Stripe)*

   What is Roscoe's problem? *(He does not manage his behavior; he wanders away.)*

3. Ask the children what they think the skill of Managing Your Behavior means. Praise the children generously for any ideas. As much as possible, tie their ideas to the following definition.

   > **Managing Your Behavior means that you try your BEST, evaluate yourself and adjust your behavior if you need to, and make sure to reward yourself.**

   Let students know that the skill of Managing Your Behavior is important to use both when you are in a group and when you are by yourself. If appropriate, direct the children's attention to the Managing Your Behavior definition poster. Leave the poster up for future reference.

4. Explain that children can use the skill when they are at home or school or in the community. They can use it right now, in their daily lives, and also throughout their lives. Ask students for their ideas about situations that require skill use. Examples:

- You are out in public with your parents. *(at the store or a movie, at a relative's house)*

- You are in a group with classmates or friends. *(in the recess line or reading circle, at lunch)*

- You are at home with your parents and brothers or sisters. *(eating dinner, watching a TV show, doing a chore)*

- You are playing with others or by yourself. *(board game, block area, playground)*

- You are working on an activity your teacher wants you to do. *(a worksheet or drawing)*

Verbally reinforce students' ideas. If you wish, record the examples on an easel pad or dry erase board.

5. Share an example of Managing Your Behavior from your own life. For instance, you might say that you use **TEAM** when you are in a teachers' meeting to listen carefully and pay attention. You evaluate yourself, and if you find that your mind is wandering, you bring your attention back to the meeting.

6. Discuss the different reasons for using the skill of Managing Your Behavior. Ask the students why they think this skill is helpful, and praise them for their suggestions. Examples:

- You will listen and learn better at school.

- You will show your parents and teachers you are responsible and trustworthy.

- You will make and keep good friends.

- You will feel good about yourself, and that will make you happy.

7. Give a general rationale for the skill of managing your behavior:

It is important to manage your behavior to show others that you are responsible.

CLOSING

1. Tell the students that they have now met Papa, Roscoe, and Roscoe's brother and sister, Bandit and Stripe. They have also discussed the meaning of Managing Your Behavior, situations in which the skill is useful, and reasons for using it.

2. Distribute crayons or markers and give students time to color pages 1 and 2 in their Roscoe the Raccoon coloring books. While they are

coloring, assess their understanding of story content and lesson concepts. Ask:

What is the main character's name? *(Roscoe)*

What is his family like? *(He has a dad, a brother, and a sister.)*

Roscoe has a bit of a problem. What is Roscoe's problem? *(He does not manage his behavior.)*

L E S S O N 2

In Lesson 1, students met Roscoe the Raccoon and his family and learned the definition of Managing Your Behavior.

In this lesson, children learn about the mnemonic **TEAM.**

In Lesson 3, children will learn that the *T* in **TEAM** tells you to try your **BEST** when managing your behavior.

TEACHING GUIDE

For this lesson, you will need a CD player, the music CD, and puppets for the Olivia, Roscoe, and Clarence characters.

1. Remind students of what was happening in the story when you left off: Papa told Bandit and Stripe that they could play by the den, but Roscoe had to go with Papa. Read pages 106–111 in the storybook.

2. Review this part of the story for comprehension, using the felt board and cutouts. Ask:

    Who is Miss Olivia? *(an owl)*

    What is Miss Olivia going to teach Roscoe? *(How to manage his behavior.)*

    Miss Olivia told Roscoe that to manage your behavior, just remember what? *(TEAM)*

    There is a sneaky coyote lurking in the brambles and bushes. What is his name? *(Clarence)*

    What do you think that sneaky coyote is up to?

3. Say, "Miss Olivia told Roscoe there are four little steps in Managing Your Behavior. Miss Olivia called these steps **TEAM.**" Tell students that **TEAM** represents the four steps of the skill:

    | T | **Try** your **BEST.** |

    | E | **Evaluate** yourself. |

| A | **Ask** yourself, "Am I doing my **BEST?**" |

| M | **Make** sure to reward yourself. |

If appropriate for your group, direct students' attention to the **TEAM** skill poster. For younger children, use the felt board and letter cutouts and go over each step verbally.

4. Use the **TEAM** song to verbally rehearse the skill steps. To do so:

    Read the lyrics on page 103 aloud.

    Have students repeat the lyrics one or two times.

    Play the song.

    Choose the appropriate puppet as each character is mentioned in the song (Olivia, Roscoe, Clarence) and pretend the puppet is doing the singing.

    Have the students sing along with the recording.

5. Ask: "Why do you think we use the word **TEAM** to help us manage our behavior?" *(TEAM helps us remember the steps in the skill.)*

6. Let students know that **TEAM** is also a reminder to be a team player when you are in a group. Explain that a team is a group of people and that being a team player means that you manage your behavior to get along with the other people in your group. Ask the children why they think that would be important. Examples:

    • You won't get into trouble.

    • You are being responsible.

    • Other people can depend on you and trust you.

7. Ask: "Where could you use **TEAM** as a reminder to be a good team player?" Examples include when doing seat work at your table and when you are listening to a story during circle time. Reinforce the children for their responses.

CLOSING

1. Tell students they have now met Olivia Owl. They know that Roscoe will learn to manage his behavior by remembering **TEAM.**

2. Provide crayons or markers and have the children color pages 3 and 4 in their Roscoe the Raccoon coloring books.

3. Assess the children's understanding of the story content and lesson concepts while they are coloring. Ask:

Who is Miss Olivia? *(an owl)*

What is she teaching Roscoe? *(how to manage his behavior)*

Miss Olivia said there are four little steps to Managing Your Behavior. What did Miss Olivia call these four steps? *(TEAM)*

Who is lurking in the bushes? *(Clarence Coyote)*

L E S S O N 3

In Lesson 2, children learned about the mnemonic **TEAM.**

In this lesson, children learn that the *T* in **TEAM** tells you to try your **BEST** when managing your behavior.

In Lesson 4, children will learn that the *E* in **TEAM** tells you to evaluate yourself.

TEACHING GUIDE

1. Remind students of what was happening in the story when you stopped reading: Olivia Owl told Roscoe about **TEAM,** while Clarence Coyote listened. Read pages 112–119 in the storybook.

2. Review this part of the story for comprehension, using the felt board and cutouts. Ask:

    What is Miss Olivia teaching Roscoe? *(to manage his behavior)*

    Miss Olivia said there were four little steps to Managing Your Behavior. What did Miss Olivia call these behaviors? *(TEAM)*

    The first step in **TEAM** starts with the letter *T.* What does the *T* tell you to do when managing your behavior? *(Try your BEST.)*

    Who taught Roscoe about **BEST?** *(a roadrunner, Rosie)*

    Uh-oh! What is Clarence Coyote up to? *(He is trying to get Roscoe in trouble by telling him about all the interesting things out there.)*

3. Reintroduce the mnemonic **TEAM,** and if appropriate, refer students to the skill poster. Remind the children that **TEAM** represents the four steps of the skill. Say, "Miss Olivia told Roscoe there are four little steps to managing your behavior. She called these steps **TEAM.**"

4. Introduce and discuss the *T* step in **TEAM.** Ask:

    The first step in **TEAM** is *T.* What does the *T* stand for? *(Try your BEST.)*

    What does **BEST** mean?

Say:

> The *T* in **TEAM** tells you to put your **BEST** behaviors forward. It's as easy as can be. You already know this skill. You use body posture *(B)* and good eye contact *(E)* to let others know you're listening. You keep a serious *(S)* face to show you're aware, and then you turn *(T)* toward the other person.

5. Give a rationale for using the *T* step. Say:

> The *T* step in **TEAM** tells you to try your **BEST.** When you do this, people will know that you are listening carefully to everything they say.

6. With another person (ideally another adult), present the skill step in the following way.

Model the Skill Step

In this and following role plays, you may model the step or steps either correctly or incorrectly at any time. If you model a step incorrectly, be sure to follow up with a correct one. (Students with cognitive disabilities may need to see correct modeling displays only.)

Choose a real-life situation that requires skill use and describe it to students: For example, you could say:

> Let's pretend that I'm sitting in class, listening to a story that my teacher is reading. A friend calls my name. I know that I need to follow the class rules. _____ is my friend. *(Have the other person whisper in your ear.)*

Model the *T* in **TEAM** by demonstrating the **BEST** skill steps.

Students Evaluate Modeling

Ask students the following questions:

> Did I do this step correctly?

> Did I do this step incorrectly?

If you did the step incorrectly, model it again, this time correctly.

Students Verbally Rehearse the Skill Step

Have students use verbal rehearsal to memorize the *T* step:

Try your **BEST.**

Students Practice the Skill Step

Ask students to describe a situation in which they can practice the *T* step. You could also use a situation you have observed recently or select one from the list of suggested role-play situations on page 101. Ask for volunteers to role-play the skill step.

Students Perform a Self-Check

After each role-play example, invite the children to evaluate performance of the *T* step. Ask:

What was good about this example?

What needs improvement?

CLOSING

1. Tell the students that they now know that the *T* in **TEAM** tells you to try your **BEST** when managing your behavior. That means using good body posture and eye contact, keeping a serious face, and turning toward the other person.

2. Provide crayons or markers and have the children color pages 5 and 6 in their Roscoe the Raccoon coloring books. Assess the children's understanding of story content and lesson concepts while they color. Ask:

When you are managing your behavior, what does the *T* in **TEAM** tell you to do? *(Try your BEST.)*

What will happen if Roscoe listens to and goes with the sneaky coyote? *(Roscoe will not be trying his BEST; he will get in trouble.)*

Do you think Roscoe will go with Clarence Coyote, or will he stay and try his **BEST?**

L E S S O N 4

In this lesson, children learn that the *E* in **TEAM** tells you to evaluate yourself.

In Lesson 5, children will learn that the *A* in **TEAM** tells you to ask yourself, "Am I doing my *BEST?*"

TEACHING GUIDE

1. Remind students of what was happening in the story when you left off: Clarence Coyote tried to get Roscoe in trouble by getting him to run off and roam. Read pages 120–125 in the storybook.

2. Review this part of the story for comprehension, using the felt board and cutouts. Ask:

   What is Roscoe learning to do? (*manage his behavior*)

   Miss Olivia said there were four little steps in Managing Your Behavior. What did Miss Olivia call these? (*TEAM*)

   The first step in **TEAM** is *T.* What does the *T* tell you to do when you are managing your behavior? (*Try your BEST.*)

   Today, Miss Olivia told Roscoe what the *E* in **TEAM** means. What does the *E* in **TEAM** tell you to do when you are managing your behavior? (*Evaluate yourself.*)

3. Discuss the meaning of the word *evaluate*. Say:

   Evaluate yourself means you ask yourself, "What am I doing?" Roscoe thought he had done his **BEST,** but he started to think about running off.

   What do you think might have happened to Roscoe if Miss Olivia hadn't swooped down and brought him back? (*He might have gotten lost or into trouble.*)

4. Give rationales for the *T* and *E* steps in the skill. Say:

   The *T* in **TEAM** means try your **BEST.** When you do this, people will know that you are listening carefully to everything they say.

The *E* means evaluate yourself. It is important to ask yourself, "What am I doing?" so you can decide whether or not you are doing your **BEST.**

5. With a partner, demonstrate the *T* and *E* steps in the following way.

Model the Skill Steps

Continue with the situation you chose in Lesson 3. For example, you could say:

The last time, we pretended I was sitting and listening to a story my teacher was reading, and I was trying my **BEST.**

Have the other person whisper in your ear. Model the **T** step.

I know I need to follow the class rules. What **TEAM** step should I use? *(Students respond.)* I need to E, evaluate myself. I ask myself, "What am I doing?"

You can model the skill or whisper back to the other person.

Students Evaluate Modeling

Ask students the following questions:

Did I do the steps correctly?

Did I do any steps incorrectly?

If you did any of the steps incorrectly, model them again, this time correctly.

Students Verbally Rehearse the Skill Steps

Ask students to use verbal rehearsal to memorize the *T* and *E* steps:

T—Try your **BEST.**

E—Evaluate yourself.

Students Practice the Skill Steps

Invite students to generate a situation in which they can practice the *T* and *E* steps, use a situation you have observed recently, or select one from the list of suggested role-play situations on page 101. Ask for volunteers to role-play the skill steps.

Students Perform a Self-Check

After each role-play example, have children evaluate performance of the *T* and *E* steps. Ask:

What was good about this example?

What needs improvement?

CLOSING

1. Tell the students they now know that the *T* in **TEAM** tells you to try your **BEST** when managing your behavior. They just learned that the *E* in **TEAM** tells you to evaluate yourself to see what you are doing.

2. Provide crayons or markers and have the children color pages 7 and 8 in their Roscoe the Raccoon coloring books. Assess the children's understanding of the story content and lesson concepts while they do their coloring. Ask:

When you are managing your behavior in a group, or when you are by yourself, what does the *T* in **TEAM** tell you to do? *(Try your BEST.)*

What does the *E* in **TEAM** tell you to do? *(Evaluate yourself.)*

What do you think Roscoe still has to learn about managing his behavior?

L E S S O N 5

In Lesson 4, children learned that the *E* in **TEAM** tells you to evaluate yourself when managing your behavior.

In this lesson, children learn that the *A* in **TEAM** tells you to ask yourself, "Am I doing my *BEST?*"

In lesson 6, children will learn that the *M* in **TEAM** tells you to make sure to reward yourself.

TEACHING GUIDE

1. Remind students of what was happening when you left off: Olivia Owl swooped down to pick up Roscoe and told him he has more to learn. Read pages 126–135 in the storybook.

2. Review this part of the story for comprehension, using the felt board and cutouts. Ask:

   What is Roscoe learning to do? *(manage his behavior)*

   Miss Olivia said there were four little steps to Managing Your Behavior. What did Miss Olivia call these? *(TEAM)*

   The first step in **TEAM** starts with the letter *T.* What does the *T* tell you to do when you are managing your behavior? *(Try your BEST.)*

   The second letter in **TEAM** is *E.* What does the *E* tell you to do when you are managing your behavior? *(Evaluate yourself.)*

   Today, Miss Olivia told Roscoe what the *A* in **TEAM** means. What does the *A* in **TEAM** tell you to do when you are managing your behavior? *(Ask yourself, "Am I doing my BEST?")*

   Olivia flew off to get a snack. Who came back then? *(Clarence Coyote)*

   What did Clarence do? *(He tried to trick Roscoe into running off to get juicy melons.)*

3. Say:

   Asking yourself, "Am I doing my **BEST?**" means thinking and asking yourself, "Am I doing each part of the **BEST** skill? Can I do something better?" You think to yourself, "Can my behavior improve?"

You ask yourself, "Is my body straight? Are my eyes on the speaker? Do I have a serious face? Is my body turned toward the speaker? Do I need to stop and not move?"

4. Give rationales for the *T, E,* and *A* steps. Say:

The *T* in **TEAM** means try your **BEST.** When you do this, people will know that you are listening carefully to everything they say.

The *E* means evaluate yourself. It is important to ask yourself, "What am I doing?" so you can decide whether or not you are doing your **BEST.**

The *A* means ask yourself, "Am I doing my **BEST?**" If you are not doing all the steps in **BEST,** then you can adjust your behavior so you are doing them.

5. With a partner, demonstrate the *T, E,* and *A* steps in the following way.

Model the Skill Steps

Continue with the real-life situation you began in Lesson 3. Model the *T, E,* and *A* steps. For example, to model the *T* step, you could say:

Do you remember when we pretended I was sitting and listening to a story my teacher was reading? What was the first thing I needed to do? *(Model your BEST behaviors.)*

Model the *E* step:

What happened next? *(Have the other person whisper in your ear.)* What did I do? *(Students respond.)* I evaluated myself. I asked myself "What am I doing?" What was I doing? *(Student responses: "You were whispering back" or "You kept trying your BEST.")*

Model the *A* step:

So what is the next step? *(Ask yourself, "Am I doing my BEST?")* Was I doing my **BEST?** *(Students respond yes or no.)*

Students Evaluate Modeling

Ask students the following questions:

Did I do the steps correctly?

Did I do any steps incorrectly?

If you did any of the steps incorrectly, model the steps again correctly.

Students Verbally Rehearse the Skill Steps

Ask students to use verbal rehearsal to memorize the *T, E,* and *A* steps:

T—Try your **BEST.**

E—Evaluate your behavior.

A—Ask yourself, "Am I doing my **BEST?"**

Students Practice the Skill Steps

Ask students to describe a real-life situation in which they can practice the *T, E,* and *A* steps, use a situation you have observed recently, or select one from the list of suggested role-play situations on page 101. Ask for volunteers to role-play the skill steps.

Students Perform a Self-Check

After each role-play example, have children evaluate performance of the *T, E,* and *A* steps. Ask:

What was good about this example?

What needs improvement?

CLOSING

1. Tell the students they now know that the *T* in **TEAM** tells you to try your **BEST** when managing your behavior and that the *E* in **TEAM** tells you to evaluate yourself. They have just learned that the *A* step means to ask yourself, "Am I doing my **BEST?"**

2. Provide crayons or markers and have the children color pages 9 and 10 in their Roscoe the Raccoon coloring booklets. Assess the children's understanding of the story content and lesson concepts while they color. Ask:

   When you are managing your behavior, what does the *T* in **TEAM** tell you to do? *(Try your BEST.)*

What does the *E* in **TEAM** tell you to do? *(Evaluate yourself.)*

What does the *A* tell you? *(Ask yourself, "Am I doing my BEST?")*

What do you think will happen to Roscoe next in the story?

L E S S O N 6

<table>
<tr>
<td>In Lesson 5, children learned that the *A* in **TEAM** tells you to ask yourself, "Am I doing my **BEST?**"</td>
<td>In this lesson, children will learn that the *M* in **TEAM** tells you to make sure to reward yourself.</td>
</tr>
</table>

TEACHING GUIDE

1. Remind students of what was happening in the story when you left off: Clarence Coyote tried to trick Roscoe into running off again, but Roscoe called out to Olivia and scooted up the tree. Read pages 136–141 in the storybook.

2. Review this part of the story for comprehension, using the felt board and cutouts. Ask:

    What is Roscoe learning to do? *(manage his behavior)*

    Clarence Coyote is sneaky. What is he trying to do? *(get Roscoe in trouble, not let Roscoe do his BEST to manage his behavior)*

    Miss Olivia said there were four little steps in Managing Your Behavior. What did Miss Olivia call these? *(TEAM)*

    The first step in **TEAM** starts with the letter *T*. What does the *T* tell you to do when you are managing your behavior? *(Try your BEST.)*

    The second step starts with the letter *E*. What does the *E* tell you to do? *(Evaluate yourself.)*

    The third step starts with *A*. What does the *A* tell you to do? *(Ask yourself, "Am I doing my BEST?")*

    Today, Miss Olivia told Roscoe what the *M* in **TEAM** means. What does the *M* tell you to do? *(Make sure to reward yourself.)*

3. Explain that a reward is something you give yourself for doing a good job. A reward can be a pat on the back, a sticker, or spending time with a friend. You can reward yourself by giving yourself something you like or need or by giving yourself praise—telling yourself you did a good job. A reward can even be just a feeling that you did something good.

Ask:

> What are some other rewards you can give yourself? *(Allow the children to express their ideas. Write the ideas down, if you wish.)*

> What kind of reward would be good for Roscoe Raccoon? *(nuts and berries)*

> What reward did Roscoe give himself for managing his behavior? *(whistling a tune)*

4. Give the rationales for all of the **TEAM** steps. Say:

> The *T* in **TEAM** means try your **BEST.** When you do this, people will know that you are listening carefully to everything they say.

> The *E* means evaluate yourself. It is important to ask yourself, "What am I doing?" so you can decide whether or not you are doing your **BEST.**

> The *A* means ask yourself, "Am I doing my **BEST?**" If you are not doing all the steps in **BEST,** then you can change your behavior so you are doing them.

> The *M* means make sure to reward yourself. It is important to make sure you reward yourself because it feels good to know that you are doing something right, and the reward will make you happy.

5. With a partner, demonstrate all the **TEAM** steps in the following way.

Model the Skill Steps

Continue with the real-life situation you began in Lesson 3. Model the *T, E, A,* and *M* steps. To model the *T* step, you could say:

> Do you remember when we pretended I was sitting and listening to a story my teacher was reading? What was the first thing I needed to do? *(Model my BEST behaviors.)*

Model the *E* step:

> What happened next? *(Have the other person whisper in your ear.)* What did I do? *(Students respond.)* I evaluated myself. What was I doing? *(Student responses: "You were whispering back" or "You kept trying your BEST.")*

Model the *A* step:

> So what was the next step? *(Ask yourself, "Am I doing my BEST?")* Did I do my **BEST?** *(Students respond yes or no.)*

Model the *M* step:

> If I decide I am doing my **BEST,** I make sure I reward myself. What could I do to reward myself for doing my **BEST** in this situation? *(Tell myself, "Good job!"; play a favorite game.)*

Students Evaluate Modeling

Ask students the following questions:

> Did I do the steps correctly?
>
> Did I do any steps incorrectly?

If you did any of the steps incorrectly, model them correctly.

Students Verbally Rehearse the Skill Steps

Ask students to use verbal rehearsal to memorize the *T, E, A,* and *M* steps:

> **T—Try** your **BEST.**
>
> **E—Evaluate** your behavior.
>
> **A—Ask** yourself, "Am I doing my **BEST?"**
>
> **M—Make** sure to reward yourself.

Students Practice the Skill Steps

Ask students to describe a real-life situation in which they can practice the *T, E, A,* and *M* steps, use a situation you have observed recently, or select one from the list of suggested role-play situations on page XX. Ask for volunteers to role-play the steps.

Students Perform a Self-Check

After each role-play example, have children evaluate performance of all the **TEAM** steps. Ask:

> What was good about this example?
>
> What needs improvement?

CLOSING

1. Tell the students they now know that the *T* in **TEAM** tells you to try your **BEST** when managing your behavior, that the *E* tells you to evaluate yourself, and that the *A* step means to ask yourself, "Am I doing my **BEST?**" They just learned that the *M* step means to make sure to reward yourself.

2. Provide crayons or markers and have the children color pages 11 and 12 in their Roscoe the Raccoon coloring books. Assess the children's understanding of the story content and lesson concepts while they color. Ask:

   When you are managing your behavior, what does the *T* in **TEAM** tell you to do? *(Try your BEST.)*

   What does the *E* in **TEAM** tell you to do? *(Evaluate yourself.)*

   What does the *A* tell you? *(Ask yourself, "Am I doing my BEST?")*

   Finally, what does the *M* tell you? *(Make sure to reward yourself.)*

   What can you hear night after night in the forest? *(Roscoe whistling a tune)*

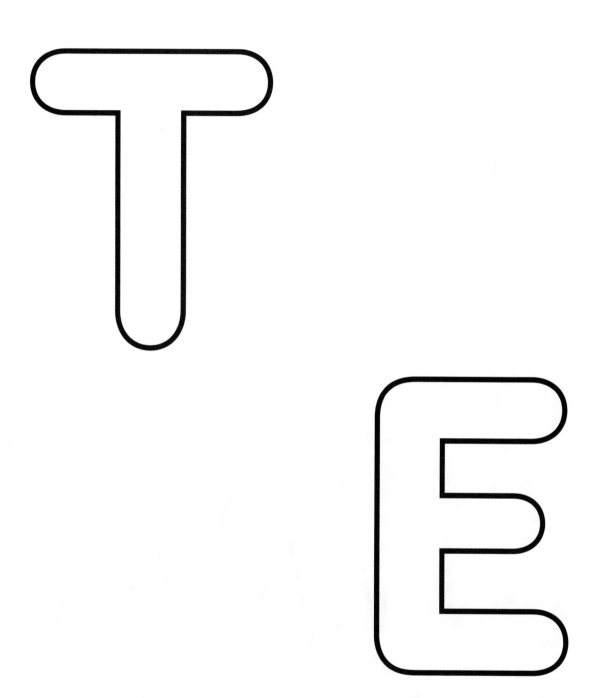

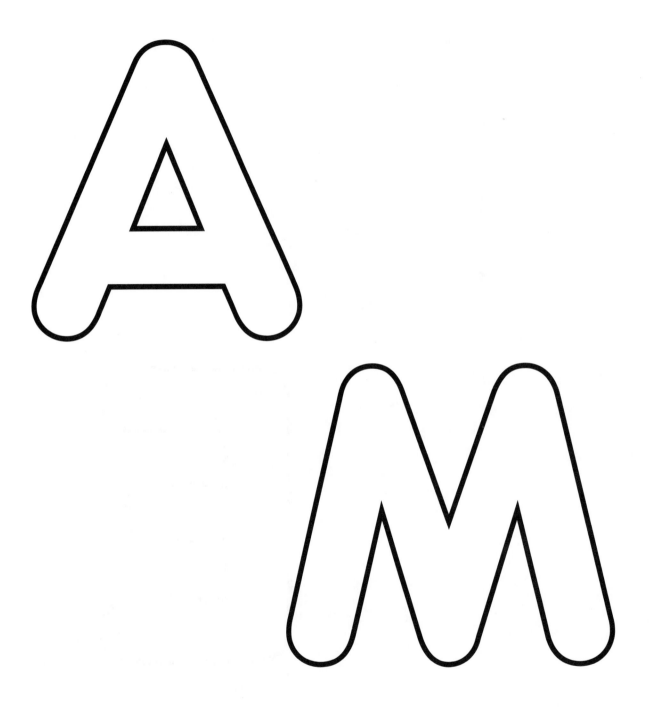

From *Social Skills in Pictures, Stories, and Songs,* by L. A. Serna, M. E. Nielsen, and S. R. Forness, © 2007, Champaign, IL: Research Press (www.researchpress.com; 800–519–2707).

Roscoe the Raccoon

From *Social Skills in Pictures, Stories, and Songs,* by L. A. Serna, M. E. Nielsen, and S. R. Forness, © 2007, Champaign, IL: Research Press (www.researchpress.com; 800–519–2707).

Papa Racoon

From *Social Skills in Pictures, Stories, and Songs,* by L. A. Serna, M. E. Nielsen, and S. R. Forness, © 2007, Champaign, IL: Research Press (www.researchpress.com; 800–519–2707).

Olivia Owl

Clarence Coyote

Managing Your Behavior

Managing Your Behavior means that you try your BEST, evaluate yourself and adjust your behavior if you need to, and make sure to reward yourself.

From *Social Skills in Pictures, Stories, and Songs*, by L. A. Serna, M. E. Nielsen, and S. R. Forness, © 2007, Champaign, IL: Research Press (www.researchpress.com; 800–519–2707).

Managing Your Behavior

T Try your BEST.

E Evaluate yourself.

A Ask yourself, "Am I doing my BEST?"

M Make sure to reward yourself.

From *Social Skills in Pictures, Stories, and Songs*, by L. A. Serna, M. E. Nielsen, and S. R. Forness, © 2007, Champaign, IL: Research Press (www.researchpress.com; 800–519–2707).

Suggested Role-Play Situations: Managing Your Behavior

1. **You and your classmates are sitting in a circle, listening to your teacher read a story. Your friends are not paying attention.**

   - What should you do?

   - Show me.

2. **You are at your table doing your math work. You are having trouble concentrating.**

   - What should you do?

   - Show me.

3. **Your teacher asked a firefighter to come to talk to your class. A friend sitting next to you is having trouble keeping still. You don't want to get into trouble.**

   - What should you do?

   - Show me.

4. **You and your classmates are waiting in line to go to the cafeteria. Your teacher said that once everyone is quiet, the class will go eat.**

   - What should you do?

   - Show me.

5. **You are in the backseat of your family car. Your family has been traveling a long time. You are getting tired, but your parent (mother or father) told you to sit still for a little while longer.**

   - What should you do?

   - Show me.

From *Social Skills in Pictures, Stories, and Songs,* by L. A. Serna, M. E. Nielsen, and S. R. Forness, © 2007, Champaign, IL: Research Press (www.researchpress.com; 800–519–2707).

Song Sheet
TEAM: Roscoe the Raccoon Learns to Manage His Behavior

Music and lyrics by L. Dennis Higgins

Lyrics
TEAM: Roscoe the Raccoon Learns to Manage His Behavior

Music and lyrics by L. Dennis Higgins

Olivia Owl, in from her prowl,
a wise old bird, so true to her word,
said, "Follow your dream,
remember to **TEAM,** and go,
hoo, hoo, hoo, hoo, hoo, hoo, hoo, hoo.
Hoot—hoot, hoot, hoot."

Roscoe Raccoon, humming a tune,
he learned from a bird, so true to her word,
said, "Follow your dream,
remember to **TEAM,** and go
hoo, hoo, hoo, hoo, hoo, hoo, hoo, hoo.
Hoot—hoot, hoot, hoot."

Clarence Coyote listened quite closely
to a wise old bird, so true to her word,
who said, "Follow your dream,
remember to **TEAM,** and go
hoo, hoo, hoo, hoo, hoo, hoo, hoo, hoo.
Hoot—hoot, hoot, hoot."

Here's what you do now,
your friends and your pals,
you don't have to guess,
you just try your **BEST**
to follow your dreams.
Remember to **TEAM,** and go
TEAM, TEAM, TEAM, TEAM.
TEAM, TEAM, TEAM, TEAM . . .

From *Social Skills in Pictures, Stories, and Songs,* by L. A. Serna, M. E. Nielsen, and S. R. Forness, © 2007, Champaign, IL: Research Press (www.researchpress.com; 800–519–2707).

Problem Solving

Prickles the Porcupine

SKILL DEFINITION

Problem Solving means deciding what the problem is, obtaining two or more solutions, recognizing the best solution, and keeping on trying until the problem is solved.

SKILL STEPS

W   **What** is the problem?

O   **Obtain** two or more solutions.

R   **Recognize** the best solution.

K   **Keep** on trying until it works.

NOTES

Underlying all of these skill lessons are the ideas that problems are a natural part of life and that learning how to solve them helps us achieve the things we want and have happier lives. To help children remember to use the skill, as you conduct the lessons you can emphasize the need to "get to work" on your problems.

L E S S O N   1

In this lesson, children meet Prickles the Porcupine, Scamper the Squirrel, and Mr. Gray Fox and learn the definition of Problem Solving.

In Lesson 2, children are introduced to the mnemonic **WORK** and learn that the *W* tells you to ask yourself, "What is the problem?"

TEACHING GUIDE

Introduce the skill by letting students know that today they will begin learning about Prickles the Porcupine and the skill of Problem Solving.

1. Read pages 143–157 in the storybook. Let students know that a *pinyon* is a kind of pine tree that grows in the Southwest.

2. Review this part of the story for comprehension, using the felt board and cutouts. Ask:

   Who are the characters in the story? (*Prickles, Mr. Gray Fox, Scamper*)

   Why is Prickles so sad? (*She can't get a hug.*)

   What did Mr. Gray Fox say to Prickles? (*She can't have any friends because she has sharp quills.*)

   Who is Prickles' friend? (*Scamper the Squirrel*)

   What is a problem? (*A problem is when things just don't seem to go right.*)

   Scamper had a problem, too. What was it? (*He forgot where he buried his nuts.*)

   How does Scamper say you might feel if you have a problem? (*mad or sad*)

   What is Scamper going to teach Prickles? (*how to solve her problem*)

3. Ask the children what they think the skill of Problem Solving means. Encourage suggestions. As much as possible, tie their ideas to the following definition:

> **Problem Solving means deciding what the problem is, obtaining two or more solutions, recognizing the best solution, and keeping on trying until the problem is solved.**

If appropriate, direct the children's attention to the Problem Solving poster. Explain that the word *obtain* means the same as *get*, so obtaining solutions means getting them. Leave the poster up where children can see it.

4. Let students know that the skill of Problem Solving is useful right now in their lives and that they will continue to use the skill many times as they get older. Ask them if they can think of situations in which they could use the skill. Examples:

   - You are having trouble with your friends.

   - Something happens at school or at home that makes you feel sad or mad.

   - You have to think about how to do something.

   - You are on the playground and can't find anyone to play with you.

   - You are fighting with your brother or sister.

   - You have to learn your alphabet letters, but you are having trouble.

   - When company visits your house, you feel as if no one is paying attention to you.

   Verbally reinforce students' responses and, if you wish, write their ideas on an easel pad or dry erase board.

5. Share an example of Problem Solving from your own life. For instance, you might say that when you are very busy at home and at school, you have to figure out solutions so you can get everything done.

6. Ask students why they think they should learn and use the skill of Problem Solving and praise them for their suggestions. Examples:

   - When you solve a problem, you will feel good about yourself.

   - Parents and teachers will be pleased that you have more control over your life.

   - If you solve a problem, it won't bother you and you won't worry or feel bad anymore.

- Being able to solve your problems will help you get the things you want.

7. Give the following general rationale for using the skill of Problem Solving:

   Being able to solve your problems will help you feel better and get the things you want.

CLOSING

1. Tell the students they have now met Prickles, Scamper, and Mr. Gray Fox. They have also learned the meaning of Problem Solving and talked about times they could use the skill and reasons for using it.

2. Give students crayons or markers and allow time for them to color pages 1–3 in their Prickles the Porcupine coloring books. As they color, assess their understanding of story content and lesson concepts. Ask:

   What is Prickles' problem? Why is she so sad? *(She can't get a hug.)*

   What is Scamper the Squirrel going to teach Prickles? *(how to solve her problem, how she can get a hug)*

   What does Problem Solving mean? *(Accept any part of the definition, then review the entire definition.)*

L E S S O N   2

In Lesson 1, children met Prickles the Porcupine, Mr. Gray Fox, and Scamper the Squirrel. They learned the definition of Problem Solving.

In this lesson, children are introduced to the mnemonic **WORK** and learn that the *W* in **WORK** tells you to ask yourself, "What is the problem?"

In Lesson 3, children will learn that the *O* in **WORK** means obtain two or more solutions.

TEACHING GUIDE

For this lesson, you will need a CD player, the music CD, and puppets for the Prickles, Scamper, Sassy, and Gray Fox characters.

1. Remind students of what was happening in the story when you left off: Scamper the Squirrel told Prickles that problems can be solved, and Prickles said she was ready to solve her problem. Read pages 158–161 in the storybook.

2. Review this part of the story for students' comprehension, using the felt board and cutouts. Ask:

   What is Prickles' problem? *(She can't get a hug.)*

   Prickles went to her friend Scamper and asked for help. Scamper said there were four steps in Problem Solving. What did she call these steps? *(WORK)*

   What do you think Prickles meant when she said she felt green? *(She felt bad or sick.)*

   Scamper said the *W* means to ask yourself something. What should you ask yourself? *(What is the problem?)*

3. Tell students that **WORK** represents the four steps of the skill:

   | W | **What** is the problem? |

   | O | **Obtain** two or more solutions. |

| R | **Recognize** the best solution. |

| K | **Keep** on trying until it works. |

If appropriate for your group, direct students' attention to the **WORK** skill poster. For younger children, use the felt board and letter cutouts and go over each step verbally.

4. Use the **WORK** song to verbally rehearse the skill steps. To do so:

Read the lyrics on page 135 aloud.

Have students repeat the lyrics one or two times.

Play the song.

Choose the appropriate puppet as each character is mentioned in the song (Prickles, Scamper, Sassy, and Gray Fox) and pretend the puppet is doing the singing.

Have the students sing along with the recording.

5. Explain that the steps in **WORK** are *nonverbal* steps, or steps you can do without saying anything. Explain:

You will want to use *self-talk* as you do these steps. This means saying what you are thinking out loud. For example, if I saw a friend crying, I might say to myself, "My friend is sad or hurt." Then I might say, "I will go see what's wrong."

As an associated activity, students can draw pictures to show what they are thinking. This approach is especially effective with younger children.

6. Introduce the first step. Say:

The first step in Problem Solving is *W*. What does the *W* step tell you to do when solving problems? (*Ask yourself, "What is the problem?"*)

Give some examples of specific questions students might ask themselves to find out what the problem is:

- Is something bothering me?

- Why do I feel sad or mad?

- Do I feel like I'm in trouble?

- What happened that might be making me feel this way?

- Does my body feel tense?

- Am I worried about something?

7. Give a rationale for using the *W* step. Say:

> The *W* step in **WORK** tells you to ask yourself what the problem is. This step is important because before you can figure out how to fix a problem, you need to know what kind of problem you are having.

8. Demonstrate the skill step in the following way. You can model the steps of this skill by yourself, using self-talk.

Model the Skill Step

In this and following role plays, you may model the step or steps either correctly or incorrectly at any time. If you model a step incorrectly, be sure to follow up with a correct one. (Students with cognitive disabilities may need to see correct modeling displays only.)

Choose a situation that requires skill use and describe it to students. For example, to model the *W* step, you could say:

> Suppose I'm in our reading circle, and someone sitting behind me keeps kicking me. I ask myself, "What is the problem?" What do you think my problem is? *(Someone is kicking you.)*

> Yes, that's right—someone is kicking me. So I say to myself, "The problem is that someone keeps kicking me."

Students Evaluate Modeling

Ask students the following questions:

> Did I do the step correctly?

> Did I do the step incorrectly?

If you did the step incorrectly, model it again, this time correctly.

Students Verbally Rehearse the Skill Step

Have students use verbal rehearsal to memorize the *W* step:

> **W—What** is the problem?

Students Practice the Skill Step

Invite students to describe a situation in which they can practice the *W* step. You may also use a situation you have observed recently or select one from the list of suggested role-play situations on page 133. Ask for volunteers to role-play the skill step.

Students Perform a Self-Check

After each role-play example, invite the children to evaluate performance of the *W* step.

What was good about this example?

What needs improvement?

CLOSING

1. Tell students that they now know that **WORK** stands for the steps in the skill of Problem Solving and that the *W* in **WORK** tells you to ask yourself, "What is the problem?"

2. Distribute the crayons or markers and give students time to color pages 4 and 5 in their Prickles the Porcupine coloring books. As they color, assess their understanding of story content and lesson concepts. Ask:

   How did Prickles feel when Mr. Gray Fox told her she'd never get a hug? *(bad, green, sick)*

   What did Scamper say **WORK** stands for? *(the steps in Problem Solving)*

   When you are solving problems, what does the *W* tell you to do? *(Ask yourself, "What is the problem?")*

L E S S O N 3

In Lesson 2, children were introduced to the mnemonic **WORK** and learned that the *W* in **WORK** tells you to ask yourself, "What is the problem?"

In this lesson, children learn that the *O* in **WORK** means obtain two or more solutions.

In Lesson 4, children will learn that the *R* in **WORK** means recognize the best solution.

TEACHING GUIDE

1. Remind students of what was happening in the story when you left off: Scamper asked Prickles what was wrong. Prickles said she was very upset because Gray Fox said that because she was so prickly, she'd never get a hug. Read pages 162–175 in the storybook.

2. Review the story for comprehension, using the felt board and cutouts. Ask:

   What is Prickles' problem? *(She can't get a hug.)*

   Scamper the Squirrel said that problems take time to work out. He also said there were four steps in Problem Solving. What did he call these steps? *(WORK)*

   Scamper said the very first step in **WORK** is *W*. What does the *W* tell you to do? *(Ask yourself, "What is the problem?")*

   Today, Scamper told Prickles about the *O* step in **WORK**. What does the *O* tell you to do? *(It tells you to obtain, or get, two or more solutions.)*

3. Remind students that the word *obtain* means the same as *get*. Discuss what a *solution* is (a way you can fix or make a problem situation better). Ask:

   In the part of the story we read today, Prickles and Scamper met their friend, the skunk. What is her name? *(Sassy)*

   Sassy had a solution for Prickles' problem. She said Prickles just might solve her problem and get a hug if she did what? *(wear a Band-Aid vest)*

Do you think that if Prickles wears a Band-Aid vest, she will be able to get hugs? Do you think Prickles has solved her problem?

4. Give rationales for using the *W* and *O* steps. Say:

> The *W* in **WORK** tells you to ask yourself, "What is the problem?" This step is important because before you can figure out how to fix a problem, you need to know what kind of problem you are having.

> The *O* in **WORK** tells you to obtain, or get, two or more solutions. This step is important because if one idea doesn't work, you'll need other ideas you can try.

5. Using self-talk, model the skill steps in the following way.

Model the Skill Steps

Continue with the situation you began in Lesson 2. Model the *W* step:

> Last time we talked about our story, I had a problem. What is it? *(Someone keeps kicking you.)*

Model the *O* step:

> That's right—someone keeps kicking me. So what do I need to do next? *(Get two or more solutions.)* Very good. So what are some ways I could solve my problem?

Encourage the children to generate solutions. Possible responses include letting the teacher know, telling the person to stop, just ignoring the other person, or even kicking the person back. If you wish, write students' ideas on an easel pad or dry erase board.

Say:

> OK, it looks like I have _____ *(however many)* possible solutions.

Students Evaluate Modeling

Ask students the following questions:

> Did I do the steps correctly?

> Did I do the steps incorrectly?

If you did either step incorrectly, model it again, this time correctly.

Students Verbally Rehearse the Skill Steps

Have students use verbal rehearsal to memorize the *W* and *O* steps:

W—**What** is the problem?

O—**Obtain** two or more solutions.

Students Practice the Skill Steps

Invite students to describe a situation in which they can practice the *W* and *O* steps, use a situation you have observed recently, or select one from the list of suggested role-play situations on page 133. Ask for volunteers to role-play the skill steps.

Students Perform a Self-Check

After each role-play example, invite the children to evaluate performance of the *W* and *O* steps. Ask:

What was good about this example?

What needs improvement?

CLOSING

1. Tell students that they now know that the *W* in **WORK** tells you to ask yourself, "What is the problem?" when using the skill of Problem Solving. They just learned that the *O* in **WORK** tells you to obtain two or more solutions.

2. Distribute crayons or markers and give students time to color pages 6 and 7 in their Prickles the Porcupine coloring books. Assess their understanding of story content and lesson concepts. Ask:

   When you have a problem to solve, what does the *W* in **WORK** tell you to do? (*Ask yourself, "What is the problem?"*)

   What does the *O* in **WORK** tell you to do? (*Obtain two or more solutions.*)

   Prickles has one solution. What is it? (*Make a Band-Aid vest.*)

   What does Prickles need to do next? (*Get other solutions.*)

L E S S O N   4

<table>
<tr>
<td>In Lesson 3, children learned that the O in WORK means obtain two or more solutions.</td>
<td>In this lesson, children learn that the R in WORK means recognize the best solution.</td>
<td>In Lesson 5, children learn that the K in WORK means keep on trying until it works.</td>
</tr>
</table>

TEACHING GUIDE

1. Remind students of what was happening when you left off in the story: Prickles wants to hurry up and make a Band-Aid vest, but Scamper says to slow down because they need to find more solutions. Read pages 176–181 in the storybook.

2. Review the story for comprehension, using the felt board and cutouts. Ask:

   What is Prickles' problem? (*She can't get a hug.*)

   Scamper the Squirrel said there were four steps to solving a problem. What did he call these steps? (*WORK*)

   The first step in **WORK** is *W.* What does the *W* tell you to do when solving a problem? (*Ask yourself, "What is the problem?"*)

   Scamper told Prickles about the *O* in **WORK.** What does the *O* tell you to do? (*Obtain two or more solutions.*)

   Prickles thought of another solution so she could get a hug. What was it? (*to blindfold her friends so they can't see her quills*)

   Why did Scamper and Prickles think this solution wouldn't work? (*It would be dangerous; someone might get hurt.*)

   Today, Scamper taught Prickles the *R* step in **WORK.** What does the *R* step tell you to do? (*Recognize the best solution.*)

   Did Prickles pick the best solution? (*not yet*)

   Why did Gray Fox say the solution wouldn't work? (*He said that everyone would want a vest and that some might not even want to wear one.*)

3. Give rationales for the first three steps in **WORK.** Say:

> The *W* in **WORK** tells you to ask yourself, "What is the problem?" This step is important because before you can figure out how to fix a problem, you need to know what kind of problem you are having.

> The *O* in **WORK** tells you to obtain, or get, two or more solutions. This step is important because if one idea doesn't work, you'll need other ideas you can try.

> The *R* in **WORK** tells you to recognize the best solution. It is important to recognize the solution that will work best so you have the best chance of solving your problem quickly and can go on and have a good day.

4. Using self-talk, demonstrate the skill steps in the following way.

Model the Skill Steps

Continue with the situation you began in Lesson 2. Model the *W* step:

> Last time we talked about our story, I was having a problem. What was it? *(Someone was kicking you.)*

Model the *O* step:

> Right! And what solutions did I obtain to solve my problem? *(Summarize these.)*

Model the *R* step:

> And how can I recognize the best solution?

> *Let students know that you recognize the best solution by thinking about what might happen if you try each one. Examine each of the solutions you have talked about. For example, if you decide to ignore the person, the person might keep on kicking you. If you decide to kick the other person back, you might get in trouble. On the basis of discussion, choose what the children feel is the best solution.*

Students Evaluate Modeling

Ask students the following questions:

> Did I do the steps correctly?

> Did I do any steps incorrectly?

If you did any step incorrectly, model it again, this time correctly.

Students Verbally Rehearse the Skill Steps

Have students use verbal rehearsal to memorize the *W, O,* and *R* steps:

W—What is the problem?

O—Obtain two or more solutions.

R—Recognize the best solution.

Students Practice the Skill Steps

Invite students to describe a situation in which they can practice the first three steps, use a situation you have observed recently, or select one from the list of suggested role-play situations on page 133. Ask for volunteers to role-play the skill steps.

Students Perform a Self-Check

After each role-play example, invite the children to evaluate performance of the *W, O,* and *R* steps. Ask:

What was good about this example?

What needs improvement?

CLOSING

1. Tell students that they know that the *W* in **WORK** tells you to ask yourself, "What is the problem?" They also know that the *O* in **WORK** tells you to obtain two or more solutions. They just learned that the *R* tells you to recognize the best solution.

2. Distribute crayons or markers and give students time to color pages 8–10 in their Prickles the Porcupine coloring books. Assess their understanding of story content and lesson concepts. Ask:

When you have a problem to solve, what does the *W* in **WORK** tell you to do? (*Ask yourself, "What is the problem?"*)

What is Prickles' problem? (*getting a hug*)

What does the *O* tell you to do? (*Obtain two or more solutions.*)

What solutions did Prickles and Scamper come up with? (*making a Band-Aid vest and blindfolding people*)

What does the *R* tell you do? (*Recognize the best solution.*)

What did Prickles and Scamper decide to try? *(making a Band-Aid vest)*

What did Mr. Gray Fox have to say about that? *(It won't work; they can't make enough; people won't want to wear them.)*

L E S S O N   5

<table>
<tr>
<td>In Lesson 4, children learned that the R in WORK means recognize the best solution.</td>
<td>In this lesson, children learn that the K in WORK means keep on trying until it works.</td>
</tr>
</table>

TEACHING GUIDE

1. Remind students of what was happening when you left off in the story: Mr. Gray Fox said the Band-Aid vest idea won't work. Scamper said that he and Prickles will need to come up with another solution. Read pages 182–187 in the storybook.

2. Review this part of the story for comprehension, using the felt board and cutouts. Ask:

   Scamper said there were four steps in problem solving What did he call these steps? *(WORK)*

   What does the **W** in **WORK** tell you to do? *(Ask yourself, "What is the problem?")*

   What does the **O** in **WORK** tell you to do? *(Obtain two or more solutions.)*

   What does the **R** in **WORK** tell you to do? *(Recognize the best solution.)*

   Today, Scamper told Prickles about the last step in **WORK,** the **K.** What does the *K* in **WORK** tell you to do? *(Keep on trying until it works.)*

   What was Scamper's new solution for getting a hug? *(tapping tummies)*

   Did Prickles solve her problem? *(yes)*

   What is Prickles wearing at the end of the story *(striped socks)*

   Children like to "hug" Prickles' way. If you wish, suggest that they give each other some Prickles hugs.

3. Give rationales for all four steps in **WORK.** Say:

   The *W* in **WORK** tells you to ask yourself, "What is the problem?" This step is important because before you can figure out how to fix a problem, you need to know what kind of problem you are having.

The *O* in **WORK** tells you to obtain, or get, two or more solutions. This step is important because if one idea doesn't work, you'll need other ideas you can try.

The *R* in **WORK** tells you to recognize the best solution. It is important to recognize the solution that will work best so you have the best chance of solving your problem quickly and can go on and have a good day.

The *K* tells you to keep on trying until it works. It is important to keep trying and come up with more solutions to your problem if your first solution doesn't work. The sooner you solve your problem, the sooner you will feel better.

4. Using self-talk, demonstrate the skill steps in the following way.

Model the Skill Steps

Continue with the situation you began in Lesson 2. Model the *W* step:

What was the problem I had? *(Someone was kicking you.)*

Model the *O* step:

Right! What solutions did I obtain to solve my problem? *(Briefly review.)*

Model the *R* step:

And what solution did I choose? *(Identify the solution chosen.)*

If you chose telling the other person to stop, for example, you could point out that this solution may or may not work. To model the *K* step, you could say:

Suppose the person keeps kicking me. What solution could I try next? *(Various responses.)*

Work through all the solutions until you and the children decide that one will work. Congratulate them on helping you solve your problem!

Students Evaluate Modeling

Ask students the following questions:

Did I do the steps correctly?

Did I do any steps incorrectly?

If you did any steps incorrectly, model them again, this time correctly.

Students Verbally Rehearse the Skill Steps

Have students use verbal rehearsal to memorize the *W, O, R,* and *K* steps:

W—What is the problem?

O—Obtain two or more solutions.

R—Recognize the best solution.

K—Keep on trying until it works.

Students Practice the Skill Steps

Invite students to describe a situation in which they can practice all the **WORK** steps. You could also use a situation you have observed recently or select one from the list of suggested role-play situations on page 133. Ask for volunteers to role-play the skill steps.

Students Perform a Self-Check

After each role-play example, invite the children to evaluate the performance of the *W, O, R,* and *K* steps. Ask:

What was good about this example?

What needs improvement?

CLOSING

1. Tell students that they know that the *W* in **WORK** tells you to ask yourself, "What is the problem?" They also know that the *O* in **WORK** tells you to obtain two or more solutions and that the *R* tells you to recognize the best solution. They just learned that the *K* in **WORK** means keep on trying until it works.

2. Distribute crayons or markers and give students time to color pages 11 and 12 in their Prickles the Porcupine coloring books. Assess their understanding of story content and lesson concepts. Ask:

When you have a problem to solve, what four steps do you think of? *(WORK)*

When you have a problem to solve, what does the *W* in **WORK** tell you to do? *(Ask yourself, "What is the problem?")*

What does the *O* tell you to do? *(Obtain two or more solutions.)*

What does the *R* tell you do? *(Recognize the best solution.)*

What does the *K* tell you to do? *(Keep on trying until it works.)*

What solutions did Scamper and Prickles think of? *(make a Band-Aid vest; use a blindfold; tap tummies)*

How did Prickles finally solve her problem? *(She got a hug by tapping tummies.)*

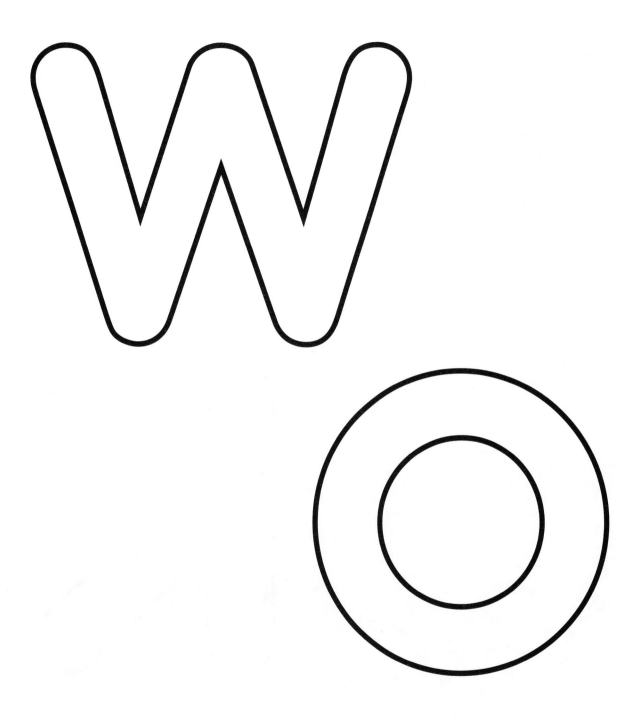

Felt Board Patterns (cont.)

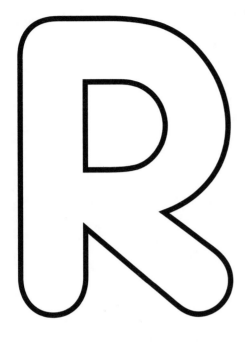

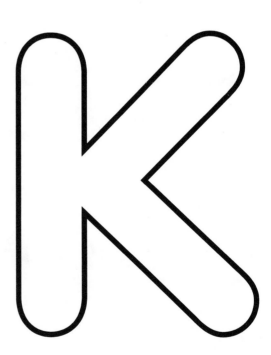

Prickles the Porcupine

Scamper the Squirrel

From *Social Skills in Pictures, Stories, and Songs,* by L. A. Serna, M. E. Nielsen, and S. R. Forness, © 2007, Champaign, IL: Research Press (www.researchpress.com; 800–519–2707).

Sassy Skunk

From *Social Skills in Pictures, Stories, and Songs,* by L. A. Serna, M. E. Nielsen, and S. R. Forness, © 2007, Champaign, IL: Research Press (www.researchpress.com; 800–519–2707).

Mr. Gray Fox

Problem Solving

Problem Solving means deciding what the problem is, obtaining two or more solutions, recognizing the best solution, and keeping on trying until the problem is solved.

From *Social Skills in Pictures, Stories, and Songs*, by L. A. Serna, M. E. Nielsen, and S. R. Forness, © 2007, Champaign, IL: Research Press (www.researchpress.com; 800–519–2707).

Problem Solving

 W   What is the problem?

 O   Obtain two or more solutions.

 R   Recognize the best solution.

 K   Keep on trying until it works.

From *Social Skills in Pictures, Stories, and Songs,* by L. A. Serna, M. E. Nielsen, and S. R. Forness, © 2007, Champaign, IL: Research Press (www.researchpress.com; 800–519–2707).

Suggested Role-Play Situations: Problem Solving

1. **You are at the store and can't find your parent.**

   - What is the problem?

   - Tell me all the ways you would try to solve this problem.

2. **You are on the playground and no one will play with you.**

   - What is the problem?

   - Tell me all the ways you would try to solve this problem.

3. **You are at school. The teacher asks everyone to get out a pencil and a sheet of paper. You can't find your pencil.**

   - What is the problem?

   - Tell me all the ways you would try to solve this problem.

4. **You are having a test in spelling today, but you are not feeling well.**

   - What is the problem?

   - Tell me all the ways you would try to solve this problem.

5. **You and your friend are not getting along. This makes you feel sad.**

   - What is the problem?

   - Tell me all the ways you would try to solve this problem.

From *Social Skills in Pictures, Stories, and Songs,* by L. A. Serna, M. E. Nielsen, and S. R. Forness, © 2007, Champaign, IL: Research Press (www.researchpress.com; 800–519–2707).

Song Sheet
WORK: Prickles the Porcupine Learns to Solve Problems

Music and lyrics by L. Dennis Higgins

Lyrics
WORK: Prickles the Porcupine Learns to Solve Problems

Music and lyrics by L. Dennis Higgins

Prickles was a porcupine, didn't have
   a friend,
had too many bristles, with very sharp ends.
Scamper was a friendly squirrel,
along with Sassy Skunk.
They worked on Prickles' problem
without much luck.

Along came old Gray Fox,
who teased with a smirk.
Sassy had an idea—
Scamper thought it might work.
"To **WORK** out your problem,
there are things that you must do.
You say you have no friends at all—
I'll prove that's not true."

So they all got together
to try to **WORK** things out,
with four steps to follow
to **WORK** a problem out.
These letters will help you, too.
Repeat what I say:
W-O-R-K
W-O-R-K...

Prickles was so happy now,
and she felt so good,
her friends could hug her—
she knew that they could.
And you could see something else,
two things that she wore—
striped socks on her feet and hugs galore.

Prickles was a porcupine, didn't have
   a friend,
had too many bristles, with very sharp ends.
Scamper was a friendly squirrel,
along with Sassy Skunk.
They worked on Prickles' problem
without much luck.

From *Social Skills in Pictures, Stories, and Songs,* by L. A. Serna, M. E. Nielsen, and S. R. Forness, © 2007, Champaign, IL: Research Press (www.researchpress.com; 800–519–2707).

APPENDIX A

Program Development and Evidence Base

The *Social Skills in Pictures, Stories, and Songs (SSPSS)* program is the result of a six-year project funded by the U.S. Administration on Children, Youth and Families and the National Institute of Mental Health. The project allowed university researchers to develop and evaluate prevention and intervention programs in local Head Start programs as part of a Head Start Mental Health Research Consortium. Four other sites besides ours at the University of New Mexico were involved in similar partnership projects: Columbia University, the University of Oregon, the University of North Carolina, and Vanderbilt University. The programs at these sites were aimed at children who were already identified as having emotional or behavioral disorders or who were in the process of being screened for such disorders. Our site was the only one targeting children who had not already been so identified. We used the four stories included in the storybook that accompanies this teacher's guide in a classroom-wide approach to teach the following adaptive social and emotional skills: following directions, sharing, managing one's behavior, and problem solving. Although the instruction was intended to prepare all children with such skills, it also provided specific assistance to children who may have been at risk for emotional or behavioral problems, possibly preventing or at least mitigating their future difficulties.

In this appendix, we briefly describe the research evidence from field trials for the *SSPSS* program and provide several annotated references for readers who wish more detail. We have arranged the first group of references, studies of our own program, in the order in which we completed the research so readers can better grasp the cumulative progression of program development and testing over the six-year period. (Over the years, the *SSPSS* program has had several titles, so readers should be aware that all refer to the same program.) We also include a shorter annotated list, arranged alphabetically, of comprehensive research reviews devoted to the general topic of social-emotional development and evidenced-based practice in this field.

Our initial study was a randomized controlled trial comparing the use of the *SSPSS* program over a 12-week period in three experimental classrooms at one Head Start preschool site. Two comparison or control classrooms at another nearby site did not receive the *SSPSS* instruction, but simply used their story time for typical preschool literacy activities. Children in experimental classrooms did significantly better than children in control classrooms, as measured by teacher ratings taken before and after the 12-week instructional period. These ratings included not only symptom lists of emotional or behavioral problems, but also measures of general social functioning (Serna, Nielsen, Lambros, & Forness, 2000). Although we taught entire classrooms and did not target specific children, scores for those few children in the experimental classrooms who were in the clinical range of emotional or behavioral disorders on the pretest (that is, were already demonstrating significant emotional or behavior disorders) were either no longer in the clinical range or did not worsen on the posttest after 12 weeks. Children in the clinical range in the control classrooms either got worse or demonstrated new behavioral or emotional disorders by the end of the same period (Serna, Lambros, Nielsen, & Forness, 2002).

A second randomized clinical trial addressed the problem of program application in the real world. In the first trial, our teacher in the experimental classrooms was a project teacher with a master's degree who co-taught the story lessons in each classroom with the local Head Start teacher. We therefore replicated the first trial with only the local Head Start teachers in six different Head Start classrooms (three experimental and three control classrooms). Our findings again favored the *SSPSS* program, but they were not nearly as impressive as those obtained in the first study. On the basis of informal observations, we did speculate that children in the experimental classrooms still seemed to demonstrate considerably more actual skill in following directions, sharing, managing their behavior, and problem solving.

We therefore undertook a third randomized clinical trial, using the exact same approach as for the second trial. However, in addition to ratings of symptoms and social functioning, we did direct, structured observations of the four skills in children from each of the six classrooms (Serna, Forness, & Mattern, 2002). We found essentially the same results on ratings of symptoms—that is, only modest improvement in children in experimental classrooms. Our direct observations, however, revealed huge differences in all four areas of skill development. In control classrooms, children demonstrated only 20 to 40 percent of the skill steps across the 12-week period. In experimental classrooms, children demonstrated 20 to 40 percent of the skill steps before the skill lessons were taught, but demonstrated 90 to 100 percent of the skill steps after the *SSPSS* lessons. These children maintained their high skill levels for the remainder of the study.

We also did a follow-up of children from our first study after four years, when they had completed third grade. Although we had difficulty locating all of these children, we managed to find a representative sample and did a systematic search of their school records. On several outcome measures related to school testing, disciplinary referrals, and need for services, children in our original experimental classrooms—those who had been in the *SSPSS* program—were doing slightly to significantly better (Forness, Serna, Mattern, Borg, Gullett, & Moses, 2003). It is also important to note that our program also appeared that same year on a list of eight social-emotional curricula having significant adoption potential for early childhood programs (Joseph & Strain, 2003).

RESEARCH ON THE SSPSS PROGRAM

Forness, S. R., Serna, L. A., Kavale, K. A., & Nielsen, M. E. (1998). Mental Health and Head Start: Teaching adaptive skills. *Education and Treatment of Children, 21,* 258–274.

This extensive review of the research literature serves as a rationale for primary prevention and universal, classroom-wide approaches to preschool mental health. It also covers developmental psychopathology, risk versus resiliency, and self-determination as bases for the *SSPSS* program and presents a rationale for selecting the four skills taught in the program.

Forness, S. R., Serna, L. A., Nielsen, M. E., Lambros, K., Hale, M. J., & Kavale, K. A. (2000). The Albuquerque YDI Head Start Program: A model for early detection and primary prevention of emotional or behavioral disorders. *Education and Treatment of Children, 23,* 325–345.

This article describes the Albuquerque Head Start program, where our research on the *SSPSS* program took place. It discusses its adoption of methods to screen for early detection of mental health disorders and the adoption of our program. It also presents preliminary data from our first year of research.

Serna, L. A., Nielsen, M. E., Lambros, K., & Forness, S. R. (2000). Primary prevention with children at risk for emotional or behavioral disorders: Data on a universal intervention for Head Start classrooms. *Behavioral Disorders, 26,* 70–84.

This article provides results of the first randomized, controlled trial of the *SSPSS* program. Three experimental and two control Head Start classrooms were involved, with a total of 53 children in the experimental curriculum classrooms and 31 in the control classrooms. Some 70 to 80 percent of children were of Hispanic origin, but all preschool teachers and Head Start staff spoke Spanish, and a Spanish-language storybook was available. We implemented the program over a 12-week period, during two three-hour periods each week. Children in control classrooms had their usual story times and literary lessons during this period, with no specific content on adaptive skills. All ten child-outcome measures used for pretest and posttest, as rated by teachers, favored children in the experimental classrooms, with five of the ten measures being statistically significant at the .04 level or better. Effect size differences between the two groups ranged from .39 to .96 on these five measures (meaning an advantage for children using our program of nearly half a standard deviation or greater over children in the control condition). The measures included two symptom ratings and three measures of social adaptation.

Serna, L. A., Lambros, K. M., Nielsen, M. E., & Forness, S. R. (2002). Head Start children at risk for emotional or behavioral disorders: Behavioral profiles and clinical implications of a primary prevention program. *Behavioral Disorders, 27,* 137–141.

This second article from our first randomized, controlled trial focuses on findings for children at clinical risk, as opposed to all children (as described in the previous article). Although our program did not target specific children, we analyzed data on just those children who met clinical cutoff points on at least three of the five measures of psychopathology used during pretesting (meaning that they met criteria for diagnosable emotional or behavioral disorders). We purposely did not identify or target any of these children specifically in our intervention. At the end of the 12-week period, however, two of these children were no longer in the clinical range, and the remaining six did no worse on any of the five measures. In the control classroom, only 1 of 31 children met clinical criteria at the beginning. This child did worse at the end of instruction, and three additional children in the control classrooms met clinical criteria on posttesting (in other words, they developed psychopathology in the absence of the program).

Serna, L. A., Nielsen, M. E., Curran, C., Higgins, L. D., & Forness, S. R. (2002, October). *Classroom-wide prevention in mental health using literacy-based materials.* Paper presented at the meeting of the Council for Learning Disabilities, Denver.

This presentation focused on the literacy and prereading aspects of the *SSPSS* and how the *SSPSS* could effectively substitute for stories included in reading or literacy curricula. Although vocabulary in the stories was geared primarily toward four- and five-year-olds, the interest level targeted a range of ages in the early childhood years. One of the co-presenters (Higgins) has also subsequently used the program with third graders with emotional or behavioral disorders, many of whom were also "twice-exceptional" (that is, classified as gifted *and* as having emotional disturbance). A University of New Mexico doctoral student in special education (Scott Gullett) recently completed his dissertation studying use of the SSPSS program in this classroom.

Serna, L. A., Nielsen, M. E., Mattern, N., & Forness, S. R. (2003). Primary mental health prevention in Head Start classrooms: Partial replication with teachers as intervenors. *Behavioral Disorders, 28,* 124–129.

This article presents the results of our second randomized, controlled trial. In this study, we made one major change. In our first trial, a university preschool teacher co-taught the lessons with the Head Start teacher. We felt that having an extra person in the classroom may have given an advantage to our experimental classrooms. In this second trial, we repeated the experiment, but only the Head Start teacher taught the lessons. We had three experimental classrooms (N = 51) and three control classrooms (N = 47). We used only eight outcome measures because two of our original ten measures seemed redundant in retrospect. As in our first study, approximately 80 percent of participating children were of Hispanic origin, with a relatively small number who were not English speakers. We also implemented a formal checklist for fidelity of treatment, which had been assessed informally during the first trial. In this study, only two of eight outcome measures were statistically significant, with effect size differences at .31 and .29 (meaning an advantage of only slightly less than a third of a standard deviation). Because this study only partially replicated our first trial, we decided to do a third trial, next described.

Serna, L. A., Forness, S. R., & Mattern, N. (2002, November). *Relationship between improvement in psychiatric symptoms and improvement in functional impairment: Data from a primary prevention program in a Head Start classroom.* Paper presented at the annual TECBD Conference on Severe Behavior Disorders of Children and Youth, Tempe, Arizona.

This presentation summarized findings from our third randomized, controlled trial on the *SSPSS* program, conducted with three experimental and three control classrooms (N = 50 and 47 children, respectively). The only essential change from the second trial, described above, is that we added four new direct outcome measures to the eight outcome measures used in the second trial. These were direct observations of the four adaptive skills. We observed skill use in each child at the end of three-week lessons on each of the four skills, over the 12-week period. As in the second trial, only two of the eight mental health outcome measures (pretests and posttests) were significant; another approached significance, all in favor of children in experimental classrooms. Our direct observations were all highly significant, however, in favor of children in experimental classrooms. For all four skills, both during baseline for the experimental students and over the entire 12-week study for controls, children demonstrated skill performance 20 to 40 percent of the time, on average. After each three-week period of skill instruction, experimental students demonstrated the skill, on average, 90 to 100 percent of the time. This finding illustrates a primary difference between mental health and school-based research in terms of outcome measures.

Forness, S. R., Serna, L. A., Mattern, N., Borg, H., Gullett, S., & Moses, M. (2003, November). *Head Start children four years later: Follow-up of preschoolers in a classroom-wide primary prevention program in mental health.* Paper presented at the annual TECBD Conference on Severe Behavior Disorders of Children and Youth, Tempe, Arizona.

This presentation described a follow-up of the 84 children who were in our first randomized controlled trial, more than four years after preschool, when these children had completed third grade. We were able to contact 21 percent of these children, but the children did not differ significantly from the total original sample of 84 on gender, ethnicity, or general functioning at the end of preschool. We then did a systematic archival records search on these 18 children over the summer and fall of their entrance into fourth grade. On several outcome measures (such as schoolwide achievement tests, school disciplinary referrals, need for Chapter 1 services, and referrals for community mental health or social services), children in experimental classrooms did slightly to significantly better. Thus they seemed to maintain gains originally made in preschool as a result of participating in the *SSPSS* program.

Joseph, G. E., & Strain, P. S. (2003). Comprehensive evidence-based social-emotional curricula for young children: An analysis of efficacious adoption potential. *Topics in Early Childhood Special Education, 23,* 65–76.

In this comprehensive review of studies of social-emotional curricula for children under six years of age, the authors selected only those programs that they considered to "have been successful in the promotion of interpersonal skills and the reduction or prevention of challenging behavior for a wide range of children . . . [based on] level of evidence or scientific believability associated with criteria that reflect efficacious adoption of curricula" (p. 65). The SSPSS curriculum was one of only eight programs selected.

Serna, L. A., Forness, S. R., & Gullett, S. (2004, April). *A story-telling intervention for young children: Five years of research.* Paper presented at the annual International Conference of the Council for Exceptional Children, New Orleans.

This presentation focused on five years of research concerning our *SSPSS* program for young children. Highlighted was a study of program use in a classroom with third and fourth graders who had emotional disorders and were gifted. The results indicated that students acquired the four skills. Generalization measures in guided and unguided situations were obtained. These results indicated that the children generalized their skill performance in both situations observed over time.

Serna, L. A., Nielsen, M. E., Higgins, L. D., & Forness, S. R. (2005, April). *Using stories and music to teach social skills to young children.* Paper presented at the annual International Conference of the Council For Exceptional Children, Baltimore.

This presentation described the *SSPSS* curriculum and how to implement its components and presented the overall findings of the project, highlighting the final study of the project. Two groups of children (experimental and control) were assessed for their knowledge of the four skills. A multiple baseline across skills design was used to assess the immediate effects of the training procedure. Results indicated that the students in the experimental group learned the skills, whereas the students in the control group did not improve their skill level over time.

RELATED RESEARCH REVIEWS

Feil, E. G., Small, J. W., Forness, S. R., Serna, L. A., Kaiser, A. P., Hancock, T. B., Bryant, D., Kuperschmidt, J., Burchinal, M. R., Brooks-Gunn, J., Boyce, C. A., & Lopez, M. L. (2005). Using different measures, informants, and clinical cut-off points to estimate prevalence of emotional or behavioral disorders in preschoolers: Effects on age, gender, and ethnicity. *Behavioral Disorders, 30*, 375–391.

This article provides a review of the literature on expected prevalence of emotional or behavioral disorders in preschool children, by way of introducing a study of 1,781 children at four Head Start sites. The study examined the effects of using several widely used measures of symptoms of emotional or behavioral disorders and several measures of functional impairment, alone or in combination, to determine percentage of children with emotional or behavioral disorders. The measures seemed surprisingly free of gender or ethnic bias, except in a few instances. Best estimates of prevalence appeared to be in the 13 to 15 percent range.

Forness, S. R. (2005). The pursuit of evidence-based practice in special education for children with emotional or behavioral disorders. *Behavioral Disorders, 30*, 311–330.

This article provides a comprehensive review of the topic of evidence-based practice in education and treatment of children with, or at risk for, emotional or behavioral problems. Evidence-based practice began in the field of medicine as a system to determine the most effective medical treatments or interventions by selecting only those treatments that met criteria for efficacy in controlled scientific studies. This practice is now being applied in mental health and education for the same purpose. The article covers what we should accept as evidence when it comes to the scientific study of interventions in these fields, how to initiate and sustain evidence-based practice, the importance of social-emotional development in young children's learning, and prevention of emotional or behavioral disorders in the early years.

Fox, L., Jack, S., & Broyles, L. (2005). *Program-wide positive behavior support: Supporting young children's social-emotional development and addressing challenging behavior.* Tampa: University of South Florida, Louis de la Parte Florida Mental Health Institute.

This monograph provides an introduction to the development of young children's social-emotional development and describes how to initiate systemwide support for such development in actual early childhood settings. The monograph has been developed with the collaboration of two of the most important national centers devoted to this topic: the Center on the Social and Emotional Foundations for Early Learning (www.csefel.uiuc.edu) and the Center for Evidence-Based Practice, Young Children with Challenging Behavior (www.challengingbehavior.org). The Web sites for both these centers provide critical information on evidence-based practices and a variety of free materials that can be downloaded on development of social-emotional skills. Just as important, these sites also provide information and materials on evidence-based strategies to use with those young children who do *not* respond to primary prevention, such as the *SSPSS* program, and who may therefore need additional, more intensive help targeted toward their specific behavioral needs.

Luby, J. L. (2006). *Handbook of preschool mental health: Development, disorders and treatment.* New York: Guilford.

This book offers a comprehensive overview of social-emotional development and specific mental disorders that may arise during early childhood, describing their causes, evidence-based treatments, and techniques for assessing such disorders. The editor, Dr. Joan Luby, is one of the foremost child psychiatrists working on such disorders and has assembled equally expert colleagues to write chapters on AD/HD, oppositional defiant disorder, depression, anxiety disorders, and related problems that may occur in early childhood. Many such children will benefit greatly from a preventative program such as *SSPSS*, but a significant number may not. Their lack of response to a prevention program effective for other children may indicate the need for more intensive intervention or referral.

Zins, J. E., Weissberg, R. P., Wang, M. C., & Walberg, H. J. (Eds.). (2004). *Building academic success on social and emotional learning: What does the research say?* New York: Teacher's College Press.

This comprehensive overview of research concerns efforts to integrate foundations for social-emotional development into academic lessons (much as we have done in the *SSPSS* program). It provides extensive theoretical and research background on the relatively new area of educational foundations and skill development.

APPENDIX B

Activities to Enhance Skill Learning

In implementing the program, we used a number of large-group, small-group, and individual activities to enhance students' skill learning. These ideas are readily adaptable; we encourage you to alter and expand on these ideas to fit the needs of the children in your own settings.

LARGE-GROUP ACTIVITIES

Vocabulary Learning

In order to prepare the children to learn each particular skill, teachers prepared activities to help them anticipate the lessons (in other words, as an *anticipatory set*). One such activity involved preparing the children for the new vocabulary that would be used in the stories. This activity especially applied to the animals that would be introduced. For example, some children did not know what a roadrunner was or what it looks like. Others did not know how the quills of a porcupine can seriously injure other animals or people.

Teachers usually introduced the animals in each story by bringing in additional pictures of the animals and talking about each animal's unique qualities. For example, they explained that a roadrunner is a bird found in the southwestern United States that can run extremely fast but does not fly like other birds. Some teachers created bulletin boards to display pictures of the animal characters as well as other aspects of the story to be introduced.

Teachers previewed the stories and chose vocabulary words that might be problematic. The following vocabulary words were introduced when we piloted the program.

> *Rosie the Roadrunner Learns to Follow Directions* **(BEST):** Roadrunner, lizard, rattlesnake, desert, cactus
>
> *Prairie Dog Pete Learns to Share* **(PALS):** Prairie dog, jack rabbit, prairie dog hole
>
> *Roscoe the Raccoon Learns to Manage His Behavior* **(TEAM):** Raccoon, owl, coyote

Prickles the Porcupine Learns to Solve Problems **(WORK):** Porcupine, skunk, squirrel, fox

Skills Book

After the children learned all the skill steps in a particular story, teachers had the children draw their own creative versions of important ideas in the story—for instance, the mnemonic BEST or what Rosie looks like when she has a straight body and her eyes on the speaker. After children created a number of pictures, the teachers stapled them together and sent them home to parents. The children were instructed to show their parents what each picture represented.

When sent home to parents, the coloring books included with this program serve much the same function as the skill books—to introduce the characters and their stories and to provide a record of the story characters and basic skill concepts. We encourage teachers to have children draw their own versions of the story characters and their adventures as well as use the coloring books. Posting children's own drawings on a special bulletin board can help them remember to use the skills.

BEST, PALS, TEAM, and WORK Songs

We found that the students loved the four songs that work as mnemonic strategies for each skill. Children would sing them in their classrooms and on the playground. To teach the song for a particular story, the teacher used the song recordings, copies of the song lyrics (for the adults), and puppets. The teacher reviewed the story with the children and then read the lyrics to them aloud. The children then repeated the lyrics one or two times. The teacher played the song, then chose the specific puppet mentioned in each part of the song, pretending the puppet was doing the singing. The children then sang along with the recording.

Role-Playing

Role-playing of skill situations took place during the lessons and individually, as a way of evaluating students' skill performance (see Appendix C). Teachers also used the following whole-group procedure:

1. All of the students stood in line, facing the teacher. Each student was called up and asked to act out the skill for the class in a task or situation provided.

2. The student performed the role play while the teacher and the other students evaluated the performance and pointed out what the student did well. If the student needed help to perform the steps correctly, the teacher provided the necessary prompts.

3. When the student performed the steps accurately, the teacher congratulated the child and gave him or her a sticker, and everyone clapped.

If students were simply unable to perform the skill at all, teachers helped them to do so at a later time, giving them the support they needed to perform each of the skill steps correctly without prompts.

Parent-Night Puppet Show

One very successful activity involved a parent-night puppet show. The show gave the children an opportunity to perform in front of their parents, and it informed parents about the skills the children were learning. In addition, the rehearsals for this show proved to be great lessons in maintaining and using the skills.

To prepare and rehearse for the puppet show, teachers created a script from sections of the story and assembled the stick puppets students had made as part of an individual or small-group activity. Teachers also obtained or created appropriate scenery (for instance, painting a desert scene on butcher paper for the background).

Teachers explained the puppet show, then allowed children to choose the character they wished to portray. Although as much as possible teachers attempted to allow the children choose their own character, they made sure to have roughly equal numbers for each character. Once the characters were established, children were assigned to different rows of chairs, according to character. For example, in the story about Rosie the Roadrunner, the following seating assignments were made:

Row 3 (back row): Lou the Lizard

Row 2 (front row): Rosie the Roadrunner

Row 1 (students sitting on the floor in front of row 2): Rosie's mom

Once the children were seated, the teachers handed out the puppets, asking the children to do their BEST while following directions. Teachers then modeled what each row of children should do in the puppet show, reciting each character's lines and showing how the puppets should move. Teachers monitored the children carefully for energy level as they rehearsed. Generally, children were able to practice their lines two or three times in one sitting without tiring. The students were ready to perform when they could say their lines without assistance.

When teachers created their scripts, they shortened the stories, making sure the dialogue they included preserved the story line. The final shows were 10 to 15 minutes long, and each show ended with the children's singing the story's accompanying song. Teachers closed the evening by serving refreshments and telling parents how they could help reinforce the skill in the home.

SMALL-GROUP ACTIVITIES

Puppet Making

To facilitate role-playing of the skill, as well as to create the puppets in the Parent Night Puppet Show, teachers had the children make puppets. In the program, we used scissors, paint sticks, tape, glue sticks, crayons or markers, and poster board, plus animal patterns like those provided at the end of each set of skill lessons. Teachers cut a number of animal patterns out of poster board and then encouraged the children to pick which puppet character they liked and color it. When the children finished coloring their puppets, teachers helped the children attach them to the paint sticks with tape.

To encourage skill generalization, teachers observed whether the children were using any of the skills they had already learned: BEST (to follow instructions), PALS (to share the crayons or markers), TEAM (to manage their behavior while assembling the puppets), and WORK (to solve problems if they arose). Teachers gave positive feedback for performance of these behaviors. When the puppets were completed, the children used them as another tool when practicing the skills as well as during the puppet show.

Clay Sculpture

Another fun activity was the sculpting activity. After the first few lessons of a skill, the children were assembled into small groups to make clay sculptures of their favorite animals in the story. Each table was equipped with clay, colored feathers, twigs, dry leaves, colorful pipe cleaners, tempera paint, and paint brushes. Teachers then demonstrated how to use the art materials. If the children needed to use black paint for Roscoe the Raccoon's stripes, for example, teachers demonstrated how to use the paint and brush. Children used feathers for Miss Olivia Owl and Rosie the Roadrunner, and twigs and pipe cleaners for Prickles the Porcupine's quills. To encourage generalization of skill use, the children were instructed to use their BEST behavior (to follow instructions), PALS (to share the paint brushes), TEAM (to manage their behavior while making their sculptures), and WORK (to solve problems as they arose). If the children were making the porcupine sculpture, they would be asked how to solve a problem using their WORK skill. Positive feedback was given with regard to the performance of these behaviors.

INDIVIDUAL ACTIVITIES

The activities next described were executed in learning centers, with each learning center having a theme associated with a skill and its related story. The goal of these learning center activities was to provide extra skill practice, using a range of materials, and to evaluate students' understanding of and ability to perform the skill. Teachers used these activities as stimuli to review a skill before evaluating students' skill performance through role-playing, as described in Appendix C.

The following types of activities usually took place at a table designated as the social skills table, where students worked one-on-one with a teacher or another adult:

1. *Felt board and felt cutouts of story characters.* Teachers encouraged students to use the felt characters to discuss the story and the skill.

2. *Clay sculptures.* Children talked about their artwork while teachers asked questions about the plot of a particular story, the characters, problems, and the skill. (Children could also discuss their stick puppets or original drawings in the same way.)

3. *Skill songs.* In addition to learning the songs as a whole group, children were given the opportunity to listen to the song recordings individually, using headphones.

4. *Skill bingo.* Teachers created bingo boards like the example on page 152, using the letters of the skill mnemonic and depictions of the animals featured in each story. Teachers called out the skill letters and animal names, and students used matching tokens to cover the appropriate squares.

5. *Skill flash cards.* Teachers made flash cards like those shown on page 153 and used them to help students review the skill steps.

Sample Bingo Board

	W	R		O
K			K	
	O	R		O
	R		K	
W		O		W

Sample Flash Cards

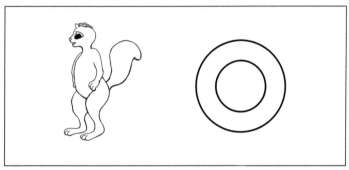

APPENDIX C

Role-Play Evaluation

In implementing the *Social Skills in Pictures, Stories, and Songs* program, we conducted ongoing evaluations of students' learning to determine whether the goals of the program were being met and what aspects of the program, skills, or instruction needed improvement. These evaluations involved collection of data on children's role-play performances of the skills and skill steps.

In our research design, we used a multiple baseline design across skills, involving multiple test probes for all skills. We also conducted evaluations of children's ability to discriminate the proper skill to use in various role-play situations. The following description offers an overview of role-play evaluation, more practical for most child care, preschool, and early elementary settings. Readers who wish more detail are referred to the research reports listed in Appendix A.

PREINTERVENTION TESTING

The preintervention testing consisted of individually testing each child prior to teaching the story/skill lessons. This testing was done to see at what level the child had the skill in his or her repertoire. We conducted preintervention test probes in one of the existing activity centers or elsewhere in the instructional classroom. In conducting these probes, teachers presented individual students with a role-play situation involving skill use, then evaluated their responses. A version of the skill checklists given following this discussion was used to record whether the child (a) exhibited the skill step as defined (a score of 2), (b) approximated the skill step (a score of 1), or (c) did not exhibit the skill step or exhibited the skill step inappropriately (a score of 0).

In conducting these initial probes, we found that some students needed to learn *how* to role-play a situation involving the skill. To clarify our expectations, we used the word *pretend* so the children would know that they should act out a situation. Sometimes we would model the role-playing of an unrelated situation. Students caught on quickly to the procedure, and we were able to assess their knowledge of the skills without difficulty.

POSTINTERVENTION TESTING

During the lessons, the children were asked to role-play specific skill steps or the entire skill, including all the skills steps. Evaluation of skill use sometimes took place in the whole group. In teaching a lesson on the skill of Following Directions (BEST), the teacher might say, for example: "Let's pretend we are doing our BEST behavior by listening to my directions about what we are going to do for recess. I want us to have body straight and eyes on the speaker. Here we go. 'All right, class, I want us to get ready for recess. . . . Good, John, you are showing me a straight body, and you are looking at me! Sally, you are doing a great job. . . .' "

Teachers also evaluated students' ability to use the skill during other classroom activities and on the playground. Teachers invited students to practice the skill. After giving feedback on skill performance in that situation, they gave students the opportunity to role-play a new situation. In this way, students had the opportunity to apply the skill in different situations, thus contributing to the generalization of the skill to multiple settings. A student's performance during these practice opportunities was considered the criterion for testing the student again more formally. When the teacher observed that a child was able to reach 100 percent of criteria in a novel role-play practice session on an entire skill, the child was eligible for a formal test session.

Once teachers determined that a student could role-play the skill steps perfectly, they used a Role-Play Evaluation Checklist for the particular skill to record the student's demonstration of the skill steps. Specifically, teachers described a novel role-play situation involving use of the skill, observed a student's use of the skill, and rated the student's demonstration of the skill steps.

Ratings were accomplished in one of two ways: In the first, teachers simply checked whether or not the student exhibited the skill during the role-play situation. In the second, they used a rating scale to assess performance of each skill. A score of 2 indicated that the student performed the skill step correctly. A rating of 1 indicated that the student approximated the skill step but needed to rehearse the skill again, with feedback. Finally, a rating of 0 indicated that the student did not exhibit the skill step or performed it incorrectly. We found the second method most accurate and reliable for our purposes.

Teachers adjusted the time allotted for evaluations to meet the learning needs of individual students; however, most evaluations took approximately seven minutes for teachers to review the skill, prompt students to perform the skill, and evaluate skill performance.

Teacher Guidelines

While conducting formal role-play evaluations, teachers followed these specific guidelines:

1. Read each role-play situation a maximum of two times.

2. Be a good listener when the student is performing the skill

3. Review the performance evaluation with the student. Together, discuss what the student did well and where he or she can improve.

4. Ask the student to identify other situations in which he or she could use the skill.

5. Follow up on the student's use of the skill outside the classroom setting.

Student Guidelines

Students were instructed to do as follows during role-play evaluations:

1. Listen carefully while the teacher reads the role-play situation.

2. Perform the skill by using all skills steps in the role-play situation.

3. Respond as if this is a real-life situation.

4. Brainstorm other situations in which he or she could use the skill.

5. Discuss whether the skill was performed outside the classroom (in other classes, at home, on the playground, and so forth).

Using Data from the Instructional Phase

If the postintervention test scores indicated that the children could perform the skill in a test situation 80 percent of the time or better, we began to teach the next skill. Before moving on to the next skill, we pretested the child again on the remaining skills that had not been taught. The next skill was therefore chosen on a stable baseline of pretest scores.

The intervention for the new skill was implemented; at the same time, the skill previously taught was reinforced in the classroom and on the playground. Once the students reached 100 percent criteria during the teaching phase of this second skill, posttesting for this skill began, as previously described. This procedure was continued for all four skills.

Role-Play Evaluation Checklist: Following Directions

Date	Student name	B (Correct posture)	E (Eye contact)	S (Serious face)	T (Turn body)	Did student follow direction?	Final score

From *Social Skills in Pictures, Stories, and Songs*, by L. A. Serna, M. E. Nielsen, and S. R. Forness, © 2007, Champaign, IL: Research Press (www.researchpress.com; 800–519–2707).

Role-Play Evaluation Checklist: Sharing

Date	Student name	P (Put BEST behavior forward.)	A (Ask yourself, "Can I share?")	L (Let the person know, yes or no.)	S (Share now or later.)	Did student share (now, later, did not share)?	Final score

From *Social Skills in Pictures, Stories, and Songs*, by L. A. Serna, M. E. Nielsen, and S. R. Forness, © 2007, Champaign, IL: Research Press (www.researchpress.com; 800–519–2707).

Role-Play Evaluation Checklist: Managing Your Behavior

Date	Student name	T (Try your BEST.)	E (Evaluate yourself.)	A (Ask yourself, "Am I doing my BEST?")	M (Make sure to reward yourself.)	Did student manage behavior?	Final score

From *Social Skills in Pictures, Stories, and Songs,* by L. A. Serna, M. E. Nielsen, and S. R. Forness. © 2007, Champaign, IL: Research Press (www.researchpress.com; 800–519–2707).

Role-Play Evaluation Checklist: Problem Solving

Date	Student name	W (What is the problem?)	O (Obtain two or more solutions.)	R (Recognize the best solution.)	K (Keep trying until it works.)	Did student implement solution?	Final score

From *Social Skills in Pictures, Stories, and Songs*, by L. A. Serna, M. E. Nielsen, and S. R. Forness, © 2007, Champaign, IL: Research Press (www.researchpress.com; 800–519–2707).

References

Forness, S. R. (2005). The pursuit of evidence-based practice in special education for children with emotional or behavioral disorders. *Behavioral Disorders, 30,* 311–330.

Forness, S. R., Serna, L. A., Kavale, K. A., & Nielsen, M. E. (1998). Mental Health and Head Start: Teaching adaptive skills. *Education and Treatment of Children, 21,* 258–274.

Fox, L., Jack, S., & Broyles, L. (2005). *Program-wide positive behavior support: Supporting young children's social-emotional development and addressing challenging behavior.* Tampa: University of South Florida, Louis de la Parte Florida Mental Health Institute.

Hawkins, D., Catalano, R., Kosterman, R., Abbott, R., & Hill, K. (1999). Preventing adolescent health-risk behaviors by strengthening protection during childhood. *Archives of Pediatrics and Adolescent Medicine, 153,* 226–234.

Luby, J. L. (2006). *Handbook of preschool mental health: Development, disorders and treatment.* New York: Guilford.

Serna, L. A., Nielsen, M. E., Curran, C., Higgins, L. S., & Forness, S. R. (2002, October). *Classroom-wide prevention in mental health using literacy-based materials.* Paper presented at the meeting of the Council for Learning Disabilities, Denver.

Zins, J. E., Weissberg, R. P., Wang, M. C., & Walberg, H. J. (Eds.). (2004). *Building academic success on social and emotional learning: What does the research say?* New York: Teacher's College Press.

About the Authors

Loretta A. Serna, Ph.D., is a professor in the Department of Educational Specialties/College of Education at the University of New Mexico. She received her Ph.D. in developmental and child psychology from the University of Kansas. Her research interests and publications are in the area of emotional-behavioral disorders, social behavior and skills, and the prevention of social-emotional problems in young children. She has developed other instructional materials in the area of social skills and self-determination skills for adolescents.

M. Elizabeth Nielsen, Ph.D., is an associate professor in the Department of Educational Specialties/College of Education at the University of New Mexico. She received her Ph.D. in educational psychology from Purdue University. Her research interests and publications are in the area of gifted education and teaching students who are both gifted and have learning or behavioral problems. Currently, she is researching the area of moral courage among children and adolescents who are gifted.

Steven R. Forness, Ph.D., is Distinguished Professor Emeritus of Psychiatry and Biobehavioral Sciences at UCLA. He received his Ed.D. in special education/psychological foundations from UCLA. From 1968 to 2003, he served on the faculty of the UCLA Neuropsychiatric Hospital, where he was also principal of its hospital school and chief of educational psychology services. Dr. Forness has coauthored or coedited ten books on children with learning or behavioral disorders and published more than 200 journal articles on special education and early detection of children with psychiatric disorders. He has received the Wallin Award from the Council on Exceptional Children and the Berman Award from the American Academy of Child and Adolescent Psychiatry.

CD CONTENTS

Track 1

BEST: Rosie the Roadrunner Learns to Follow Directions (2:58)

(Song sheet and lyrics: page 40)

Track 2

PALS: Prairie Dog Pete Learns to Share (3:16)

(Song sheet and lyrics: page 68)

Track 3

TEAM: Roscoe the Raccoon Learns to Manage His Behavior (3:23)

(Song sheet and lyrics: page 102)

Track 4

WORK: Prickles the Porcupine Learns to Solve Problems (2:56)

(Song sheet and lyrics: page 134)